Surviving Miscarriage

Surviving Miscarriage

✦

—You Are Not Alone

Dr. Stacey J. McLaughlin,
Licensed Psychologist and
Miscarriage Survivor

iUniverse, Inc.
New York Lincoln Shanghai

Surviving Miscarriage
—You Are Not Alone

iUniverse books may be ordered through booksellers or by contacting:

iUniverse
2021 Pine Lake Road, Suite 100
Lincoln, NE 68512
www.iuniverse.com
1-800-Authors (1-800-288-4677)

ISBN-13: 978-0-595-35636-2 (pbk)
ISBN-13: 978-0-595-80111-4 (ebk)
ISBN-10: 0-595-35636-2 (pbk)
ISBN-10: 0-595-80111-0 (ebk)

Printed in the United States of America

Contents

1

Introduction

Are you fearful that you may miscarry, or have you recently suffered a miscarriage? Are you waiting for test results from your doctor to know for sure? If so, you are not alone—millions of women miscarry every year. Miscarriage is one of the most misunderstood tragedies that a woman can experience, and many women suffer in silence. You don't have to.

"I can't seem to stop thinking about how far along I'd be if I hadn't lost the baby, and I can't help wondering whether it was a boy or a girl."

I am Dr. Stacey McLaughlin, and this book contains my story as both a woman who has lived through two miscarriages and as a professional psychologist. I have written this book because of my deep desire to help women like you and their loved ones—to let you know that you are not alone.

Feeling Misunderstood and Alone

Perhaps those closest to you have never experienced a miscarriage, and thus have very little idea of what you are feeling or how to help you. This is perfectly normal, although it is extremely frustrating.

Following a miscarriage, we are often forced to go back to work, where we have to deal with colleagues who don't know what to say to us. They may offer condolences, trying to be kind, but these condolences only serve to remind us of our pain or make us feel uncomfortable. We are then forced to go home to our other children, who want to know where Mommy's baby is. Next, we are forced to call friends and family members to cancel the baby shower plans and tell them to return any baby gifts they may have bought. We have to stop decorating the nursery and buying baby clothes at every store we enter.

You are probably feeling a sense of emptiness and isolation right now, but it's important for you to know that other women out there can empathize with you fully. Others, like me, have gone through this, too, and they can help you get through it.

Above all, remember that you do not have to deal with this agony alone or pretend to put on a happy face for the benefit of those around you. You do not have to deny your feelings. Recognize them and address them in order to move on and heal yourself.

The pain of miscarriage is something that many women bear by themselves, but this usually only worsens the situation. In isolation, pain is never fully healed. Women who deny their feelings and try to cover them up are forced to get on with their lives without fully dealing with their loss. That deeply embedded pain just gets harder and harder to handle over time.

An Unspoken Aspect of Women's Lives

Another very difficult aspect of miscarriage is that we women are very rarely taught about it, what to expect, how to handle it, and so on. It is a part of life that is often very hidden and discreet—until it happens to you. Then you become hit full-force by something you probably never expected, something you may not fully understand.

I know, because I went through it myself. I personally never knew how hard it would be, both physically and emotionally, to have a miscarriage—let alone two miscarriages—until it actually happened. I was not prepared at all, and I was therefore very poorly equipped to cope with the tremendous emotions and sadness I felt. What I experienced was a pain I wish no one would ever have to go through, but I know now that it's something many, many women experience.

My intent in writing this guide is to give others, like you, the benefit of my own experience and to make sure that the pain is not compounded by uncertainty, unawareness, ignorance or lack of information. Yes, this is a tragic event, one that none of us would wish on our worst enemies. Yet, if anything can help make it a little better, it is the certainty of knowing exactly what we are going through, the knowledge of what to expect and the tools to teach us how to cope.

Once you begin the process of experiencing a miscarriage, or once your doctor informs you that you may be miscarrying, it is difficult to know where to turn or who to talk to. Should we call our spouse or significant other right away? Should we call our boss to let him or her know that we may be missing work? Should we call our mothers for support and guidance? Should we call our friends so they can come over and cry with us?

Often, the first person we turn to when we hear the bad news is our doctor. This has both a positive and negative aspect, since doctors can be full of information but may also lack emotional support. While some physicians are wonderfully skilled at helping women through this painful experience, others may unwittingly become so focused on the medical side of the miscarriage that they ignore, minimize or even trivialize the emotional side of it. It can be a shock, but even your ob-gyn may not be as understanding or caring as you want or need during this critical and stressful time.

If this is your experience it may be tempting to get irate or depressed over your doctor's reaction, but this does not help anyone, least of all you. Please keep in mind that physicians are a crucial part of the healing process, and that their very profession forces them to focus on the physiology of the miscarriage, not the emotional aspect. Your doctor wants to see you get better just as badly as everyone else in your life, but they need to concentrate on what they know best: your body.

When you miscarry, your body goes through a terrible ordeal. A doctor's job is to monitor you to make sure you are healing properly. This physical recovery is just as important and crucial to your health as is the emotional recovery. Moreover, a doctor can give you plenty of concrete information about what your body is experiencing, how to help yourself, and how to understand what has happened to you.

That said, if you are not pleased with how your doctor is handling your situation, please discuss this with him/her or find another doctor. It is essential that you surround yourself with friends, family members, and professionals whom you can count on and trust to help you in your healing.

If you put yourself in capable hands and surround yourself with a support system, and if you commit yourself mentally to recovery, you will surprise yourself by how strong your spirit is and how much better you are going to feel just a short way down the road.

The Road to Recovery

I want you to know that it is okay and perfectly normal to feel hopeless—for a time. I understand what it is like to feel utterly alone (even when you are surrounded by friends and family) and despondent, and I know that it is necessary to allow yourself to experience those emotions in order to eventually release your anger and sadness.

I also want you to know that there *is* hope. I know it for a fact. I am living proof that no matter what life holds for you, no matter what your future may look like, you *will* survive. The challenges and hardships you face can either defeat you or make you a stronger person in the process. I am here to say that even if you feel anything BUT strong today, there is always the opportunity to turn tragedy on its head and come out of it a tougher, wiser, more resilient and dynamic human being!

More than most other women out there, I empathize with your pain—and I know what it will take to overcome that pain and find your happiness again. It is this empathy and this firsthand knowledge of your situation that has led me to write this book. I don't want other women out there to be stuck in a prolonged depression after a miscarriage, unable to get their lives back on track. I want to share my story with you to help you understand that you are not alone and that this pain, too, shall pass.

I am also writing this book because my two miscarriages have given me a wealth of knowledge about this often unspoken subject in women's lives. Since I had never been told much about miscarriages, and since I didn't know what to expect or how to deal appropriately with what I was experiencing, I went out and did my own research. The difficulty of this process made me realize that women like you and me were being underserved and ill informed.

When I went out there to search for my solace, I found that the Internet, libraries, and other resources available to me only focused on healthy babies or women who had had horrible tragedies. Very little of that was applicable to my situation. There was almost nothing out there for women like me who had suffered one or two miscarriages. At a time when I badly needed information, support, and understanding, it was a tough battle to dig up the knowledge I was after. That, in turn, only made me feel more alone.

One of the ways I learned to heal myself was to turn to women like you, women who had also experienced miscarriage and could enlighten me with their knowledge and advice. I learned that what I was experiencing was normal, and I also came to understand that miscarriage was not uncommon, and that many others had gone through exactly what I had just gone through.

Through my discussions with other women, I learned that women who already had children often felt misunderstood, too. They felt that they didn't have the right to grieve or suffer the pain they experienced because they were already mothers. In the words of one woman:

"I have just had a miscarriage, at 12 weeks. I am finding people's reactions strange, as I have 3 lovely children, ages 16, 14 and 11, and this baby was a surprise to my husband and I, as we are both 40. There will probably be no 'next time' for us, which really saddens me now. I am fed up with being told, 'Well, at least you have 3 healthy children.' I know this, but am I wrong to have wanted 4 healthy children? I am finding no support for some-one my age who has 3 kids and was expecting a later-in-life baby. I just can't believe I'm not pregnant anymore and still rub my tummy without think-ing. Then, of course, I cry again. Hopefully this will stop soon."

If this is your situation today, please take comfort in the knowledge that you DO have the right to grieve just as much as anyone! And if you are having trouble finding the right support in your close circle of friends and family, you can always find it here, and on the Internet.

Many of you who are in a similar situation, whether or not you already have other children, have submitted your stories to our website. I have included many of your comments, with permission, in this book so that you will know that you are not alone.

One of the common comments I hear from women who have suffered through miscarriage is epitomized in the words one reader posted on the site:

"What I need most is, as you put it, to come out of this 'secret' group of bro-ken souls. Validation & belonging go a long way to healing & this is such a lonesome journey right now. How do you get support when others around you don't see your pregnancy as a 'real' child?"

One way to get that support is to seek out women who know what you are going through. It is very hard for someone who has never had a miscarriage to be able to sympathize with your unique and powerful feelings. That's why I've put together this book, which contains both my story and stories from many other women out there. It is my sincerest hope that this book will give you comfort, by letting you know that what you are experiencing is normal.

My Story, and How I Hope It Will Help You

My book starts out with my story—and I leave nothing out about the pain, heartache, and suffering I experienced. I, too, suffered the comments of well-meaning friends who wanted to help but had no concept of what to say, which only made things worse. I felt the pain of watching friends and relatives nurture their healthy children, wracked by the envy and anguish of knowing that mine had not survived. I want to share this story with you so that you can nod along and say, "Yes, that happened to me, too! So I'm not the only one whose husband or friends or mother or boss seemed insensitive! So I'm not the only one who felt envious of my best friends and their beautiful families!"

Before the guilt, envy and pain, of course, I underwent a great deal of strange, new and frightening events that I was not entirely sure how to cope with. I have therefore included a chapter in this book on how to cope with the uncertainty of not knowing whether or not you have miscarried, and what tests you will likely face. I explain how to take care of yourself during this stressful time, and what you can expect while waiting.

In the cases where miscarriage is recommended and not a natural occurrence, I also discuss the option of choosing a D & C procedure to speed up the process. Each choice has pros and cons and is an individual decision. It is therefore my goal to arm you with enough information for you to make a wise decision that is appropriate to you, your life and your individual situation.

Next, I discuss the five stages of grief as described by psychiatrist and author Elizabeth Kubler-Ross. Let no one tell you otherwise: a miscarriage is a death in your family, and these five stages of grief apply to you as much as to anyone else who has lost a loved one or is facing the loss of his or her own life. It is therefore important for you to recognize and understand the five stages of grieving, and to go through each stage on your way to recovery.

Of course, what makes your situation different and more difficult than that of someone who has lost a parent or a spouse, for example, is the lack of memories you have with the child your body nurtured from conception. You are left with the knowledge that you will never know what kind of person he or she would have grown up to become. This is a terrible thought to live with, but it is one that all women who miscarry seem to share:

> *"We lost our baby of 9 weeks 2 days ago. I am 40; my youngest child being 16 years old, this child was a welcomed blessing in our home. We only knew that we were pregnant for 2 weeks before the loss.... just grasping the concept that our lives would change and we would be sharing it with a new little one, the kids were already discussing names and activities.... The pain is undeniable, and the loss is so real...And now we realize we really want a little one in our lives."*

It is a sad thought, but it is a normal and healthy one. In my book, I'll show you how to express this feeling in a healthy way, as well as ways to embrace this grief and then let it go.

Sadness comes hand in hand with events like miscarriages, but there is a boundary between appropriate grieving and dangerous depression. In this book I detail the symptoms of depression and anxiety so that you can recognize them and know when and how to reach for help if they become overwhelming to you. I also provide suggestions for self-help during this stage of grieving. In our society, no one really ever teaches us how to deal with our deepest and most difficult emotions; this book is an attempt to educate you about your sadness, your grief, your disappointment, so that you can master and overcome those feelings in the end.

I also discuss the troubling issue of "child envy"—feeling envious of those friends of yours who have children. Throughout your pregnancy you have probably been imagining your own tots playing with your friend's children, or what it's like to be a mother just like your best friend or sister. Now that you have miscarried, you will probably be wondering how to handle the loss of that vision. You may be uncertain about how to cope. Should you carry on like nothing happened? Should you tell your friend, sister, etc., that you just couldn't bear to be around them and their children any longer? Can you recover without isolating yourself from your friends with children forever, while knowing that it is okay to take a break from them when the pain is most intense? This can often be a very painful and real dilemma, especially since the very friends you need most for support can be your most significant source of pain if they have healthy children.

Much of this book is devoted to how to take care of you in the aftermath of a miscarriage. This means learning to say "no" to the well-meaning friends and relatives who don't understand that you may just want to be alone at times. This also means learning how to forgive friends who say things that hurt you, like, "The child probably would have been deformed anyway," or, "At least you already have one healthy child." I'll also show you how to find small ways of experiencing happiness when you are ready to do so. In addition to emotional care, this book also discusses the physical side of things, too: continuing to take your prenatal vitamins if you don't know for sure that you have miscarried, getting adequate rest, and so on.

I'll also tackle the difficult but critical issue of how your relationship with your spouse or significant other may be impacted by a miscarriage. Many of you may at this very moment be feeling abandoned or misunderstood by your husband, boyfriend, or partner. You may be finding that his/her way of dealing with the situation is much different than your way—the two ways of coping don't have very much in common. This, again, is normal; everyone deals with loss differently.

That's one of the reasons why our significant others often seem to allow some magic amount of time in which we can grieve our loss before finally "moving on." Still, we may find ourselves under pressure to "try again" before we are ready to. On the flip side, when we ourselves want to "try again," we may find ourselves met with great resistance; perhaps our significant others are "too scared" to give it another go.

This part of the healing process is very much about the two of you—your relationship—and is not just a one-sided issue. In the middle of our grieving, we are forced to make decisions we are often not ready to make—like whether we want to try to conceive again, whether we should look into adoption, or whether we should abandon the idea of children all together. I was faced with many of these very issues, and that's why I have devoted a chapter to them, especially for the benefit of your partner or significant other. I provide many suggestions about how they can best help you, and also about what *not* to do to avoid making you feel alone and/or pressured.

Finally, I discuss the decisions most commonly faced by women who have recently miscarried, as well as a guide to how to make the best decisions for you. I want to stress, however, that it is perfectly okay to take all the time you need to heal before making any major decisions that will affect you, your family, and your life. Do NOT allow yourself to be pressured to try for another child, to adopt, to move, to buy a new car, or to make ANY decision that requires your full attention until you have moved through the pain of this very real tragedy in your life. Making a decision based on pain, depression, sorrow, anger, resentment, envy or guilt will not give you the contentment you crave right now.

So give it some time. Whatever you eventually decide regarding parenthood is okay. It is your decision to make, after all—but it's a decision that should wait until you are ready to make it with a clear head and a strong heart.

Above all, I have written this book for you as a way to give you answers you may not be able to find anywhere else, to provide personal stories for you to identify with, and to make this common but tragic event a little less mystifying and terrifying. When you think about it, other kinds of grief are commonly written about in books, newspapers, magazines, and so on. People talk openly about, say, losing an older relative. In a situation like that, it seems that everyone knows what to say. They remind you that he or she has lived a full life, and that you have many precious memories shared with this person that will live on in your mind.

When you lose an unborn child, however, it can feel like no one knows what to say—and as a result, you have none of the comforts you would have in other circumstances. Miscarriage is one of the most isolating events a woman can experience, and my book is an attempt to bridge the gap and provide you with comfort that was not available to you before.

> *"Evidently I have no problem with fertility, but an inability to sustain a pregnancy beyond 8 weeks or so. My sadness is cradled by my continued hopes to become a mother…so I find myself, two days after the d & c that helped my body finish the process nature had begun, optimistic that through intensely managed care with my obgyn practice…that there will indeed be LIFE at the end of this dark tunnel."*

Remember, no matter how gloomy things may seem now, you will get past it, and you do have hope. I have been there, and I want to do my best to help you along on your road to recovery and a healthy new outlook on life. Let's embark on this journey together, with all the benefits of shared experience and a common understanding of an event that may have changed your life but should never destroy your spirits.

2

My Story

Before my first miscarriage, I hardly even knew what the word meant. I'd heard it before, but I knew nothing about the emotional and physical scars a lost pregnancy could leave. I didn't know the ways it would affect my husband and me, not to mention those around me.

In retrospect, I am positive that my confusion and lack of awareness about the perils of pregnancy made things harder for me than they would have been otherwise. I hope that by reading my story you can come to understand some of what you are going through, and that you can relate to the events, emotions, and challenges of my own experience.

My Background

Before I begin my story, I'd like to start off by giving you some background information. As I mentioned earlier, I am writing from the perspective of someone who has experienced miscarriage, and from the point of view of a practicing psychologist who has helped many people dealing with loss. I live and work in Central Florida, and have been for many years. Mine is an incredibly rewarding and fulfilling career, and I have no regrets.

In order to build my career, however, I postponed both marriage and having children in order to finish my bachelor (B.S.) and doctoral (Ph.D.) degrees in psychology from Florida State University. I also worked for two years between my undergraduate and graduate degrees. It was not until I was in my 30's that I finally felt it was time to marry my wonderful husband, Chris. As many women are postponing families for their careers in our modern times, I do not feel that my background is unusual in this respect. In fact, I think of my experiences as being pretty common in this day and age, something that helps me relate to many of my patients.

The First Miscarriage

In short, I was happy to devote my life to my education and my career for a time. But once I got married, I felt that I had waited long enough. Putting my personal life second for all those years only made me that much more anxious to make the decision to move forward with having a family. As soon as we got married, therefore, my husband and I began thinking about what our life together would be like with the addition of a child.

I remembered my mother telling me how hard it was for her to get pregnant; so Chris and I decided to start a family right away. It actually didn't take very long at all before I conceived, and we were able to announce our pregnancy as of January 2003. We were thrilled and excited—we could hardly wait to tell our friends and relatives. We began thinking about our future, our unborn child, and his or her life with us, and how our household would change. I loved looking into the future and imagining how different things would soon become.

Our excitement and joy were short-lived, however. Ten weeks in, I went in for a check-up, when I got the bad news. The doctors could not detect the baby. It was simply no longer there. The doctors attributed my condition to something called a "blighted ovum." They said it was a "chemical pregnancy"—a pregnancy in which the fertilized egg just dissolves. But the rest of my body didn't know the egg had dissolved, and so it had generated a gestational sac, just as though I were still pregnant. To make matters worse, my Hcg (pregnancy) blood levels were continuing to rise. This made it difficult for the doctors to diagnose a miscarriage and we were asked to return for more blood work and ultrasounds for two weeks until we were certain there was not a baby anymore.

I was devastated and confused. The doctors told me that no one knows why blighted ova or chemical pregnancies occur, but rather than making me feel better, that only made the situation more frustrating and difficult to accept. I kept thinking to myself that if there was at least a good reason for all this, maybe the lost pregnancy would be easier to handle—but there was no reason, and I had no justification.

My body was still carrying its gestational sac, and I chose to miscarry naturally to end the pregnancy for good. As I suffered actual labor pains and contractions over the course of several days, I grieved terribly for the loss of my child.

It was during this time that I began to approach the "experts" for the support I so desperately needed, but no one really seemed able to understand the emotional aspect of my experience. No one could empathize with what I was feeling. I felt isolated and lonely, trapped by my emotions and my sense of loss.

I was also very worried about the prospect of getting pregnant again. Would I be able to conceive as easily this time? Would I be able to carry the baby to term? Would I have another "chemical pregnancy"? What would I do if I miscarried again? I terrified myself by imagining the worst—that I would not be able to have a normal baby.

I decided to go back to my doctor and ask for tests to find out if anything was wrong with me, if anything was keeping me from having a normal pregnancy and a normal baby. However, my doctor suggested that I hold off on any testing for the time being. She told me that I would have to try again, and that if I ended up miscarrying three more times, then she would see about the testing. The health professionals I consulted with in follow-up to my doctor simply told me to wait three months and then continue trying to get pregnant.

Another situation made my already painful situation even worse. One of my sisters-in-law conceived at the same time I did, and she ended up carrying a healthy baby to term. I have a hard time articulating the clash of emotions I felt: the loss of my own baby, the happiness for my sister-in-law, the jealousy of her "normal" life, and the guilt that I had not been able to do what she had done. To this very day, I still look at her baby and think about how old my child would have been if she or he had survived. I am also overwhelmed by a love for her child, almost as if she were my child. Her little girl is so special to me and even more so because of the timing of her birth.

At that point in my life, I felt utterly empty. I had begun envisioning my new life as a mother, and now it had been taken away from me. I had wanted so badly to bring a new life into the world, and now my baby was gone. It was going to have been my first pregnancy, and now the joys of a young marriage were tainted by tragedy and sadness.

Then there were the people in my life who knew I had been pregnant, and to whom I had to give the bad news. It was awful, humiliating, depressing and stressful to go to them and say, "I miscarried." Some of them seemed to think that 10 weeks was not much time, and that I could hardly have grown attached to my baby by then. Others just said, "You're young, you have plenty of time." Some of my family and friends did help me out a lot, but many of them just made me feel worse.

To add to that, my husband seemed uncertain of how to act, and I don't blame him. This was a turn of events neither of us had ever anticipated, and we were both devastated and confused. One of the things that helped me later on was discovering that other women, too, experienced a similar feeling of distance from their spouses after a miscarriage. One woman told me:

"Being my first pregnancy, I had told all my family and friends before the 1st trimester was over. I did not know back then that you were supposed to wait before telling anyone…so everyone knew. We had to call everyone and tell them I had miscarried. During this time, I was upset with my husband because he was spending more time with his friends watching football and playing video games. That was one of the hardest things to endure."

The Second Miscarriage

Three months went by slowly, during which time I became more and more hopeful. I reasoned that I had already had my bad luck, and it was not likely to happen again. In June, we made the decision to try again, and I once again felt full of hope, expectations, dreams and visions of my future as a parent.

This time around we were much more scientific about the process. We even used an ovulation predictor kit faithfully! We did everything by the book, and by August we were pregnant again. Needless to say, both Chris and I were extremely happy. We were ready to put behind us the pain of what had happened last time around, and instead to embrace our new future with our unborn child.

This time, however, our hopes were dashed after only six weeks. By that point, my baby had no detectable heartbeat, even though my HCG levels (which are supposed to double every 72 hours) were perfectly normal! The baby was still there, the doctors could detect it, and I had a gestational sac, too. There was just no heartbeat.

When the doctors told me that my baby was no longer living, I was absolutely devastated. Once again, I felt the anguish of a lost pregnancy, but I also felt the agony of having been through this before, fearing that I would have to go through it again. Just as I had done before, I was forced yet again to go through the physical pain of a natural miscarriage while enduring the emotional pain of losing yet another baby.

To make things worse, I miscarried on the same day as my husband's 30th birthday party. It was extremely difficult for me to watch him being in so much pain over this and yet wanting to help me. I also knew that he was not sure what to do or say to help me. I wanted desperately to reach out to him—to help *him*—but felt that I was empty inside and had nothing left to give. That caused me even more pain: the feeling that I was somehow failing in my role as his partner, even though I knew in my heart that I needed time to grieve for myself.

My husband went back to work the next day, and my mother and mother-in-law came to stay with me during my dark hours. Chris needed to throw himself into work to lessen the pain, while I needed to grieve and confront my feelings. I did not understand then how my husband could return to a "normal" life right after such an abnormal event, but I do understand it now. He was grieving in his own way, and it didn't mean he wasn't hurting. Indeed, he was hurting very much.

If you find yourself in a similar situation, as do many women out there, it is important to realize that your partner or significant other may cope with loss differently than you do. This is perfectly okay. In fact, it's more likely than not that the two of you will have different reactions—human nature involves individual responses and unique behaviors. Don't expect others to feel the same way that you do, or to act in exactly the same way. And take comfort in the fact that your spouse's different perspective may actually help you look at your loss in a new light. Your differences can actually be beneficial to both of you, by giving you a broader outlook on your experience.

I also discovered that finding some joy and laughter, even in my darkest hours, was a way to recover and get through my grief. One of my best girlfriends became pregnant a little while before I did, and I ended up planning her shower while going through my own miscarriage. Of course, the baby shower was yet another painful reminder of my loss, but it was also an important chance to step outside of my grief for a moment. Looking back, I realize that only wallowing in my own sorrow would have really created a dangerous situation. But by making an effort to help someone else, I was able to get out of my head for a moment and take part in my friend's great joy.

That girlfriend continues to be a wonderful friend to this day, and her daughter is a bright ray of sunshine in my life. I will always be proud that I was able to share in my friend's joy—something I was not always able to do with others during the period following my miscarriages.

While I did sometimes need the support of others, however, there were definitely times when I just needed to be alone. Being with friends and family gave me a support system, but I found that they often wanted me to talk about myself, to express my emotions, to discuss what had happened. In fact, I got so sick of people asking me to tell my "miscarriage story" that I actually thought about writing it down and handing it out for people to read, so that I wouldn't have to keep repeating it. Trust me, you will only be able to tell your "miscarriage story" so many times before you just can't tell it anymore.

Moreover, when others were around, I had to drop my denial and admit that this had really happened to me. Whenever I saw their sad faces and their concerned expressions, I remembered my loss. I answered their questions and told them my story, never able to just let it go for a moment and think about something else. Only when I was alone could I drop the subject.

Adding to my stress during and after both miscarriages was the fact that my job required me to be able to help people. Because I could not put off going back to work forever I didn't get much time to recover before I had to function as a psychologist again, pushing my own pain aside.

As many of you will discover, it is extremely difficult—if not impossible—to concentrate on anything else while you are grieving the loss of your child following a miscarriage. Unfortunately, most of us have jobs that do not allow the luxury of grieving while we're working. We have to concentrate on the tasks before us, chatting with our colleagues, meeting with clients and so on. We have to stay "on the ball," not letting our minds wander. Therefore, at work we have to put aside our problems. This is so tough for anyone who has recently experienced a tragedy like a miscarriage, which can keep playing over and over again in your mind.

What Was Wrong?

Following this second miscarriage, I demanded to know what was wrong. Why had I miscarried again? My doctor had previously told me that she would hold off on testing until I had miscarried several more times, but now I absolutely refused to wait any longer. I wouldn't allow the doctors to tell me that I had to endure this agony again before finding out what was wrong. So, for the next five months we underwent extensive infertility testing at a specialty clinic.

During these five months of uncertainty, I obsessed in my mind about what had caused my miscarriages. I imagined every possible scenario and revisited all my habits. Was it the sushi I liked to eat, the party I had attended right before learning I was pregnant, the crazy hours I worked? Was I to blame, or was it my difficult heredity, given the tough times my mother had had while trying to get pregnant? Had I waited too long to start a family?

It is so easy to start blaming yourself for the miscarriage without knowing exactly what the root cause is. I know this, because I did it to myself, over and over. I caution you not to beat yourself up too much. Rarely are miscarriages our fault; we just have to suffer the pain. This is the worst part, in my opinion. Even though we have done nothing to cause the miscarriage, we still have to deal with the loss.

In addition to enduring the testing itself, I also had to suffer through the holiday season. I was already being poked, prodded, and examined like a melon in a grocery store—I did not need any more stress. Well, I got it anyway. My sister-in-laws all have children: one has three, and two have two each. As I have already mentioned, one conceived at the same time I did for the first time, and she had already delivered her healthy baby. Every time I saw their children I wanted to cry. Even worse, while all my relatives were very supportive, as were my friends, I sensed that all secretly had fears that this could happen to them, too. My loss was like the elephant in the room—the thing that no one wanted to look at or talk about, but which everyone was thinking about.

As a psychologist I know firsthand how difficult the holidays can be for people, even in the best of circumstances. The stress can sometimes be more than people are able to deal with. If you have to go through the holidays during a miscarriage, you may find that you have additional stresses, making an already unpleasant situation even harder. When you are physically and emotionally unable to function in family gatherings, it can be really tough.

Personally, I found myself caught between two extremes: wanting to protect and take care of myself, and wanting to help my family deal with my miscarriage. I know they didn't all understand what had happened, and they were worried about me and how I was handling the miscarriages. On the one side, I just wanted to grieve and be sad, but on the other hand I wanted to put on a good face so that my family wouldn't suffer, too. That made for a very rough holiday season.

> *"Though I try to not slip in the abyss of despair, sometimes my emotions and humanity get the best of me. I am often the one to comfort my family—I guess this is a natural instinct—because I don't want them to worry about me."*

My Search for Solace

During both of my miscarriages, I felt so depressed, so low, so anguished, that all I wanted was for someone to say something, anything, that was profound enough to make me feel better. I was constantly disappointed when nothing anyone said seemed to help me. Later, however, I came to realize that my desperate hopes and my eventual disappointment were very normal and to be expected. But even this realization only added to my loneliness. I had come to understand that, just as my experience was intensely personal, at least some part of my pain had to be endured alone. That was just the way it had to be. It wasn't that I wanted it to be that way—it just was what it was.

Eventually, when I was ready to hear what people had to say, I found that certain things really helped. The point is that it only began to make sense to me when I was ready to hear it. I would have been even more devastated had no one tried to reach out and comfort me with words at that time, when I was so desperately in need of help.

My message to you is this: let your significant other, your family and your friends know that they shouldn't stop trying to help you even if you push them away at first. Distance is part of the grieving process, but it will soon come to an end. Eventually you will need your support system, and they will need to be there for you!

> *"Unfortunately, a lot of people don't understand how it feels. The only people who do are those who have been there…"*

I also found that, in addition to wanting to be alone at times, I became isolated from those who didn't want to be around me in the aftermath of my miscarriages. A few of my friends with children chose not to speak to me about their children, creating a sense of isolation in our friendships. I knew that these friends wanted to talk about their sons and daughters, but that they were making a conscious effort to avoid those painful topics.

Other friends went in the opposite direction, pushing their children on me as an effort to make me feel less "empty" or "alone" or "childless." Some tried to get me to "take Johnny for a day"—thinking they were helping me, when they were actually only making me feel worse.

However your friends react, keep in mind that they are not trying to be hurtful on purpose. They are merely trying to spare your feelings and to help you in the best way they know how. This is such a tough time for others around you. No one knows what to say, not even you, but people still want to help make it better. They all care about you and are worried about you, and their efforts are usually a sign of love and compassion.

If it feels right now that everything only drives the pain deeper, and that nothing is going to make you feel better, don't despair. One day soon you will wake up feeling happier. Once you get to that point, you will greatly appreciate the many comforts that your friends will give you.

For that time when I did not find much solace in friends or family, I turned to other sources. I began to search feverishly for answers, visiting the library, surfing the Internet, shopping at the local bookshop. All my efforts were largely in vain. I found very little material out there about my experience. It was very frustrating, to say the least.

As I mentioned earlier, the only resources I had available to me seemed to feature happy stories about happy, healthy babies or else horribly tragic stories that had nothing to do with me. There was no happy medium, no in between. There was no book, no resource, no information about women who have had one or two tries at pregnancy and one or two or more miscarriages, and who feel terrible about losing their children.

I drove myself crazy trying to find someone or something to relate to—but the harder I searched, the more I realized how taboo this subject really is. People don't like to talk about miscarriages. We talk about heart disease, the deaths of parents or grandparents, romantic woes, but even the best of friends do not often share the deep pain that is associated with losing a baby.

When I came to this realization, I could scarcely believe it. So many women miscarry and no one talks about it! How can this be? Wouldn't women want to share their experiences, to help one another, to create a support system of people who know what you are going through? I was so disappointed and frustrated by the lack of available information and resources for women like me.

I kept searching everywhere for help and found very little, which was astonishing because, as a psychologist, I know where to look for reliable information. I can safely say that I did a very exhaustive search on this topic, and still turned up very little at the end of it all. All I can say is that it is just not fair that there exists such limited information about a topic that affects so many women.

> *"I am 21 years old. I'm in the Army and was recently stationed in Iraq with my fiancé. I found out I was pregnant and was medically re-deployed back to the States. I was 13 weeks when I went in for my ultrasound, and the doctor told me my baby didn't have a heartbeat. I was devastated, confused, angry, and guilty. I was afraid to tell my fiancé and my family what happened because I thought they would blame me for doing something wrong and causing this. This was 2 days ago, and since then I've been on the internet all day and night doing research trying to find out all I can about miscarriage. I'm so frustrated, because all the sites I have visited offer no more than a text book explanation of what the cause of it is."*

I didn't know what I needed. Sometimes I wanted to read positive, upbeat and hopeful stories. At other times I just wanted to wallow in my pain. At still other times I gravitated to the most tragic, horrible stories I could find, just so I could make myself feel that at least my tragedy wasn't as bad as other people's. This had the strange effect of giving me relief while I was reading these awful stories, then making me feel guilty for using someone else's tragedy to make myself feel better. Even worse, these tragedies made me even more frightened about my own family and our future. In the back of my mind I could not help thinking that these could still end up being my story—there was still time.

I remember, for example, watching a television show about a woman who had ten miscarriages. I cried all the way through the show—not just because of the grief I felt for this woman, but also because of my underlying fears that her story could one day become my story. I could not stop myself from worrying that my miscarriages would not end with two.

I also found myself comparing my life to the lives of my friends and family members. Maybe I didn't realize that I was doing it at the time, but I saw it in retrospect. I had a tendency to gravitate toward my single friends who were eager to be married. They would talk about how they were lonely and how there were no great guys out there—and I would silently console myself with the fact that I at least had a great husband (or at least a husband who was great most of the time!). Later I would feel a bit ashamed of being happy about my friends' shortcomings (or what they saw as their shortcomings). But at the time, I was just doing everything I could to keep myself from falling further and further into a pit of despair.

You never want to fault anyone for their happiness, of course, but it is really hard to feel like you're the only one suffering. It's so difficult when it seems like everyone around you is experiencing nothing but happiness. But remember, that is often just how things *seem*. The way things actually *are* can be quite different if you scratch below the surface.

The grass is always greener—isn't that always the case? When you want to be in a relationship, all you notice are happy couples. When you want to have a child, all you notice are other women's children. It's because your own energy is so focused on that one need or want that it becomes all you see. It's a psychological phenomenon I've become very familiar with—and you've probably grown familiar with it, too.

Communicating Without Guilt

Whatever your reaction, whatever the responses of those around you, and however you embark on your path to solace, it all starts with the recognition that miscarriage is an emotionally isolating and trying time. It can be especially difficult when the reactions of those around you are not always empathetic or helpful.

I personally found it tough to learn to deal with people or things that were standing in the way of my own solace, but soon I figured out a way to make my situation easier. As time progressed, I learned to recognize the things that helped. I spoke up and let the people around me know when they were helping, because I wanted them to keep doing those positive actions. This ensured that I always had some beneficial support around me to help get me through the worst times.

I also learned to speak up and let people know when the things they were doing were NOT helping me at all. I know that many of us are taught to "say nothing if you don't have anything nice to say." But suffering in silence can make an already tough time even harder to endure. Speaking up and letting others know how you feel is an important phase of your healing, and you should not skip it out of fear of not being "polite." I definitely suggest that you learn to communicate your feelings without guilt. Your speaking up will most likely be appreciated. After all, the people who care for you probably don't know what to do to help you, and they need your guidance.

What I Hope You Will Take Away From My Story

So there you have it—my story, what I experienced, how I coped with the people around me, how others coped with me, my research efforts, my search for solace, and some tips I learned along the way.

I don't expect that you will have exactly the same experience as me, but one of the things I want to keep stressing in this book is that miscarriage does not have to be something you suffer alone, silently, in the dark and without any help or knowledge about your situation. As I learned myself, that kind of response to a tragic event is apt to make things worse for you, as well as for the people around you.

What helped me, and what I hope will help you, is to know that the people around you are probably just as worried, confused and unsure of the proper response as you are. You should also realize that everyone has a different reaction to events like these. Surround yourself with people you love and who love you. No matter what their response is, you will know that you can be honest with them, whether that means telling them you just need to be alone or asking them for help. Remember, you will get through this. If I did, you can, too.

3

How to Cope during the Period of Uncertainty

Have you gone to your regularly scheduled doctor's appointment recently and heard the words, "There is a problem here"? Did your doctor tell you that your HCG levels are not where they should be, or that he's having trouble finding a heartbeat?

This is what I call the period of uncertainty. It's a moment or a period of time in which you just don't know for sure whether you still have a healthy baby or if you have miscarried. It is probably going to be one of the toughest times you will face in your life—I know it was for me.

I wish I could tell you that it will pass quickly, but the fact of the matter is that it may last for as long as several weeks. Please be prepared for this—it will likely take some time before you get any definitive answer from your health professional. I was not expecting that, and I found it extremely frustrating. I honestly don't know what is worse: going in for a regularly-scheduled doctor's appointment and being told that you have lost your baby, or going in for a regularly-scheduled doctor's appointment and being told that the doctor does not know what is going on. Both are devastating. It's definitely no picnic to be confused, upset, sad and worried—and on top of it all to have to go in for weeks of blood tests and ultrasounds.

And the uncertainty is not just confined to confusion about what is actually going on in your body. It can also extend to your confusion about what the doctor is looking for, what the tests are looking for, and whether or not there is a deeper medical issue. I personally have never loved going to the doctor to begin with, and I don't know many people who do. It's always slightly uncomfortable and confusing to have someone probing and prodding your body—especially because many of us aren't that well-educated when it comes to our anatomy and what's going on in there. As one woman told me:

"I wish I had had a better understanding of what the tests really mean. Some women are not good at asking doctors for details—and some doctors aren't good at giving the details. Especially when it comes to additional testing or advanced medical techniques, I have heard so many stories and am not sure what the truth really is."

First of all, I want all of you to know that while I am a psychologist, I am not a medical doctor. The best source of any medical information is and will always be your medical doctor. The information provided in this book is based on my own experiences and research and is meant to be a guide to help you figure out what questions to ask and what information to gather about your situation.

As you will soon understand, many women experience miscarriage, but each experience is different and sad in its own right. That means that each situation also has its own particular medical issues, involving particular tests and procedures. Your doctor will do what is right for you and what is appropriate given your unique circumstances.

How to Know if you May Be Miscarrying

Many of you have written to my website concerned about whether or not you are miscarrying, and sharing your stories about when you learned that you might be or were miscarrying. The following is just one of the emails I have received:

"In May 2004 my husband and I decided I would go off of the pill, and by July I was already pregnant. I got pregnant so quickly I didn't even realize I was pregnant until August. By the time I got a pregnancy test I showed 6 to 8 weeks, and when the Doctor checked me he thought I was about 10-12 weeks. It turned out I was pregnant with twins!

"However, by the time I had my first ultrasound, I had lost both of them. My husband and I were both devastated. In November-December I was told we could start to try again if we felt up to it. We had been trying ever since without a positive.

"Then, in January, I felt very definite pregnancy symptoms. On Saturday I went to the doctor for a blood test....it was positive. By the end of the day I started to bleed, but still with no cramps. I called my doctor and he thinks

miscarriage is happening or has already happened. I am supposed to rest and go back in Monday.

"At this point, I don't even know how to cope. I don't even know if I can bear to go to the doctor on Monday. I am crushed."

This sad email brings up a very common question: How do you know if you are miscarrying?

Even if you are not aware that you are pregnant, symptoms such as breakthrough bleeding, excessive cramping, or passing tissue or large clots can mean that you are miscarrying—but such symptoms are not always indicators of miscarriage. Often, when the embryo is attaching itself to your uterine lining, bleeding (light or heavy) can occur.

Sadly, once the symptoms I've listed above begin, there is not much that the doctors can do except just wait and see. Many physicians will recommend bed rest and abstinence from intercourse or heavy exercise. Some will also recommend a special diet. But for the most part, at this point doctors are hesitant to say that you are miscarrying—which is appropriate. Many women have bleeding, even excessive bleeding, and go on to have healthy pregnancies and healthy children. So please keep in mind that bleeding alone does not mean that you are miscarrying. It is a symptom of miscarriage, but not always.

If you are pregnant and have any questionable symptoms, it is critical to go to your doctor immediately! Your doctor can perform an ultrasound and pelvic exam, and those tests will in many cases give you some answers. They will usually be able to show whether you are indeed still pregnant and whether the baby still has a detectable heartbeat.

My doctor used to tell me that once a heartbeat is detected, miscarriage rates drop significantly. I can remember so vividly going into my doctor's office and sitting through numerous ultrasounds, just holding my breath to hear if there would be a heartbeat or not. I know exactly what it is like to wish so strongly for a heartbeat, only to hear or see none. This is so devastating—trust me, I know what it's like. I would not wish that sort of pain on anyone.

Once again, the best source of any medical information is your doctor, or doctors. If you are experiencing anything that could be construed as a symptom of miscarriage, the first call should be to your physician. He or she will be able to interpret your symptoms and help guide you to a diagnosis.

That said, if you really feel that your doctor is wrong or is not helping you enough, you should always feel free to ask for a second opinion about your case.

Know that this is well within your right as a patient. Now is not the time to worry about hurting your doctor's feelings. There is a lot at stake and there is no room for error.

Blood Tests—What to Expect Initially

Based on my experiences, I can give you a good idea of what to expect once you begin the testing. It will be frightening, but one thing that really helped me was having knowledge about what to expect from the ordeal. Having that knowledge gives you at least a little sense of power, especially in the midst of a situation in which you can so often feel completely powerless.

Once a problem has been detected, the doctors will subject you to a series of ongoing blood tests. One test will look for HCG, or "human chorionic gonadotropin." This is a hormone produced by the placenta during pregnancy; home pregnancy test kits use it to determine whether or not you are pregnant. A general rule of thumb is that your HCG levels should double every 48-72 hours, although this is not an exact rule. Your doctors will measure these levels to see if they are increasing normally or not.

I want to take a moment here to caution you all to take everything you read on the Internet regarding what is "normal" for HCG levels with an enormous grain of salt! There is a lot of misinformation on the Internet. Here are the facts: most doctors will base what is normal for you on YOUR prior HCG levels, not some table of numbers. All you need is for your HCG numbers to increase or double. That is all. The bottom line is, every woman's levels are different, and so you really should not compare your levels to anyone else's levels. If you do, you will only succeed in driving yourself crazy with worry, and for no good reason.

> *"My first miscarriage was in August of 2004. I never seemed to have any problem getting pregnant, but the first baby died at 9 weeks. We discovered it during an ultrasound. Then the doctors watched my HCG level for a week, and they dropped. Afterward I had a D&C.*

> *"The second time I got pregnant I went in for an ultrasound at 9 weeks, but the baby only measured 6 weeks and the sack was 8 weeks. They checked my HCG levels and did a 2nd ultrasound 3 days later. At that point we could not see a baby and the HCG levels had dropped, so I had a D&C again. Now I wonder if I will ever be able to carry a child to term."*

When you go in for blood testing, you will probably be visiting the doctor or lab every day or every other day—sometimes for weeks on end. At this point, you will be faced with some practical decisions—do you want to go alone, or do you want to bring along your partner, your mother, your friend? When is the most convenient time for you to make these trips? These are the obvious logistical questions, and you should take the time to answer them honestly for yourself. Don't bring along someone who isn't good moral support, but don't feel that you have to go alone and suffer that anxiety all by yourself. It can often be a good idea to have someone there to help distract you from time to time.

Then there is another important question which people rarely think about ahead of time: where do you want to be when the doctor's office or lab calls to tell you the results of the latest tests? You really need to be in a place where you can experience an appropriate reaction without embarrassment if you get bad or unexpected news. Hearing that your levels have dropped or have stayed the same would be very difficult for someone who is working in an office with little privacy.

To get around this problem, I suggest telling the nurses that you want to call them, and that you don't want them to call you. Arrange a mutually convenient time, and then make sure to call at the designated moment. You should make sure that you have the appropriate support network around you, and that you are in a place that allows you to react normally (your home, a friend's house, etc.).

You Will Not Have Immediate Answers

"My miscarriage experience has been a hard one. My HCG levels have gone down and then back up during this process. I wonder if anyone else I know has ever heard of this happening. It has made it hard on me to grieve. After my hormones went down the first time, the doctor told me I was having a miscarriage. I started to let go of my baby even though I still feel pregnant and haven't started bleeding yet.

"Four days later, however, I went in to have my blood tested again only to find out three days later that my hormones were back up to around 280. They then told me to come in ASAP for an ultrasound and another blood test, only to find out later that night that the my levels had dropped to 180. It has been an emotional rollercoaster.

"I'm supposed to go in about 5 days for another test. At this point I don't know if I should give up hope that my baby is still alive or just accept what the doctors say and accept that I'm having a miscarriage. It's been so hard for me because I haven't started bleeding and I still have pregnancy symptoms."

It is human nature, especially in our modern society fueled by "instant gratification," to want to know what is going on right away. We never want to wait; we want answers NOW. Unfortunately, when it comes to medical matters this is most likely not going to happen. In order to endure the ordeal, you must learn to manage your frustration appropriately, which starts with expecting a bit of a wait in most cases.

Adding to this almost inevitable frustration is the fact that most doctors do not know why most miscarriages happen. Even with the most rigorous testing, the reason why can remain a mystery. Perhaps it is something as simple as a blood-clotting problem, or an incompatibility between the sperm and the egg—but again, for a time you are probably not going to know the root cause.

I personally employed a number of strategies to keep myself occupied and to get my mind off the pressing matters at hand as much as possible. I learned that it really does help to occupy yourself with work, family, or other things that you find enjoyable. I highly recommend structuring your days so that you are not free for long periods of time, during which you could wind up excessively worrying about the baby. Try to surround yourself with other people, or give yourself activities to do. Read a great book, watch your favorite movie, get a stack of magazines, and so on. Just be sure to have enough to do so that you don't find yourself staring off into space and getting anxious.

After all, as your doctors will probably tell you, there is really nothing you can do at this point but wait. You need to remain on your prenatal vitamins, and you should be sure to follow any orders your doctor gives you. Some of you may be placed on restricted activity or bed rest, and if you are, it's important to stay calm and avoid exerting yourself. But other than following these instructions…it really is just a waiting game. It is a very tough, emotional game, so keep your loved ones close and remember to give yourself lots to do (again: books, TV, movies, music, and so on).

Of course, the scenarios I've just described won't apply to everyone out there. Some doctors, upon not hearing the fetal heartbeat, will want to rush you into an ultrasound to find out what is happening. This may appeal to your desire to know RIGHT NOW, but it can also have a really devastating impact, even worse than if you had had some time to prepare. For example, I have a good friend who went alone to what she thought was just a routine checkup for her pregnancy. However, the doctor found something wrong, and my friend ended up getting rushed into an ultrasound. The doctor saw right away that the baby had died, and my friend ended up learning that she had lost her baby—while she was vulnerable, scared, unsure of what was going on, and alone.

Remember: IT IS YOUR BODY, and you have the right to choose when and where you find out the truth. You don't have to let the doctor rush you if you are not ready to hear what he has to say. You can always go into the lobby and call your partner or a friend on your cell phone. You can ask someone to meet you at the doctor's to give you moral support. You can even make an appointment to come back later for another appointment, when you will be more prepared to receive the news.

My Advice on How to Handle this Difficult Period

"On our first try, we got pregnant! I was elated and my husband was just floored with happiness. 5 weeks into our pregnancy, however, I started to spot heavily. Though this can be 'normal,' I called my doctor, and he asked me to come in for a check. When they did the ultrasound and the blood test, they found that the baby was the size of a 2-week-old and that my progesterone level was at 364. My hopes were crushed."

As you await the news, you are most likely feeling a certain level of stress. But you are also probably getting ready to experience a significant amount of even worse stress, both physically and emotionally. I empathize totally, and I feel that the best way to prepare is simply to hear from someone else who has been through it what you can expect.

In my experience, the stress of waiting for the news is tougher than most of the kinds of challenges we face in the rest of our lives. This is because these feelings are just about the complete opposite of what you expected to feel when you first found out that you were pregnant. You probably expected, as did I, that you would do nothing but laugh and smile for the next nine months, rubbing your belly and eating ice cream.

Now, however, you are starting to learn the harsh reality that being pregnant is not always so full of contentment and joy. It can also be full of uncertainty, or nervousness, or worry and doubt. You are also realizing that, having gone through the beginning stages of pregnancy, you will have to switch gears instantly if you find out you are miscarrying. Instead of feeling that you are at the beginning of something wonderful, you will start to realize that you are at the end of something tragic. That switch is so tough to make, and it may leave you feeling nothing but numbness or disbelief.

I remember vividly what it was like for me. I was going to my first doctor's appointment at the start of my pregnancy, and I was so very excited about the baby. I had so many questions to ask and such high hopes. I even wore a brand-new outfit to fit with my new dreams and my new life as a mother.

Before then, it had never even crossed my mind that I would leave that appointment in tears, struggling to figure out what had happened. In one short moment, I had gone from thinking of myself as a new mother to knowing that I was no longer carrying the child I thought I was. It was excruciating.

> *"I just lost a baby 3 days ago. I was 5 months pregnant. I just had an ultrasound on Dec. 29th and everything was fine, and a few days later I started to realize that I hadn't been feeling her kicking at night. How could something go wrong in just a few days? I had to go through the whole labor process, which just about killed me. I just don't know if I can go on, and I have a 2-year-old to take care of. I know it is probably normal to feel the way I do, but I just feel like I will feel this way forever."*

Finding out that I was miscarrying was a huge stress in my life, maybe the biggest I have experienced up to this very day. Chances are that this may be the biggest stress that you, too, will have endured in your entire life to date. If not, then you have a great resource from which to draw upon. What other painful or stressful experiences have you had in your past that you were able to conquer or overcome? Think back to what worked and what didn't work during this prior difficult experience or experiences. You will probably find that whatever helped you then may also be a great help to you now.

In particular, try to remember whether you healed from being around others or from being alone. Did you benefit from the wise words of a parent or a relative? Did you find solace in being surrounded by friends? Perhaps you were able to heal that past stress by either diving back into work or taking some time off and going on a much-needed vacation.

You may also want to think about how you cope with more minor stresses on a daily or an occasional basis. Do you tend to deal with stress better by journaling about your life, putting it down on paper as a way to "talk it out" with yourself?

Or does it help you to simply take a break from your thoughts for a while, doing something to get your mind completely off the matter at hand?

Remember, there are no wrong answers here. Whatever has helped you before is likely going to do you a lot of good now. Whatever it was that you did to help make it through the pain and difficulty you experienced earlier in your life, try it again now.

At the same time, also try to think of what actions or behaviors have made stress worse for you in the past, and then avoid them. Be extremely careful about any dangerous coping skills, like drinking, overeating, gambling, or excessive spending. This is not the time to engage in unhealthy activities, no matter how badly you feel. They will only make you feel worse—I guarantee it.

If you are not sure of what might help you through this difficult time—ask your friends what they do to help themselves. I've learned firsthand that you can get some great ideas from other people. Different people have different coping methods, and you may be pleasantly surprised by the vast number of ways that people have come up with to deal with the stresses in their lives.

As for me, I discovered a few activities that almost always did the trick. I went to a lot of movies and often walked around a local lake. I also cooked gourmet meals for my husband, taking a long time to chop the ingredients well and to cook from scratch—this intensive work kept my mind fully occupied. I enjoyed driving to the beach for the scenery, too. Though it was a tough job sometimes to get myself motivated to leave the house, I knew I needed to. Every time I felt myself obsessing—waiting by the phone, doing research on miscarriage on the Internet—I would fall back on one of my tried-and-true activities. They helped keep me sane during a very trying time. After all, a person can only spend so much time waiting by the phone.

That is how I coped, but you should find your own set of enjoyable activities. Do what you really love to do, because you will need to occupy yourself in ways that are meaningful to you. Please do not worry about whether or not you are being too self-centered or taking too much time for you. Weathering this storm means deciding how you want to be nurtured for the next several weeks—you deserve to take care of yourself.

Accordingly, you will need to make some decisions about how to spend your time. Do you want to take some time off work? If you have other children, do you feel like lining up some babysitters? If you have a lot of activities or obligations, do you think you can stick to them all, or should you consider streamlining your calendar? Don't feel badly about canceling social obligations during this time—you have to think of yourself first!

You also have to decide how much attention you need. It may sound funny to think about planning this in advance, but it really is an excellent way to make sure you are taken care of in your moment of need. Some people want to be alone, and some need their friends more than ever. I had a different friend call and check on me every night, which really helped. Of course, I'm not talking about having all your friends and family rush over to spend hours and hours by your side. When my friends called me, we spoke only for a few minutes, just to say hello. That was all I needed. These calls were just to let me know that people really cared about me and how I was doing.

There is another aspect of this time period that you may not be anticipating. As your body will be entering a "fight or flight" stage, you can expect to either be sleepless or wanting to do nothing but sleep. Either response is perfectly normal; you just need to go with the flow, doing whatever feels natural for you. I will spend more time later on discussing how to know when too much sleep or a lack of sleep becomes problematic. However, at least initially, for the time being, know that it is okay to let your body grieve, as it needs to.

Some women find that they have a strong need to be pampered at this time or to pamper themselves. This is perfectly fine just so long as it coincides with your doctor's recommendations. If you have been put on bed rest, stay on bed rest. Now is not the time to be running around town. And even if you are feeling depressed and hopeless about your pregnancy, this is not a good time to revert back to pre-pregnancy habits like overindulging in drink or giving up those pre-natal vitamins. You would feel terrible if your doctor ended up telling you that your baby was fine and you had done something that could possibly have harmed your unborn child.

Instead of any potential dangerous activities, just stick to whatever provides you with a healthy, natural sense of peace and strength! If you are an extroverted person, you may need to be surrounded by friends; plan a home-cooked dinner or a movie night in your living room. If you are a detail-oriented person, having a sense of structure and order in your life may help; sit down and write up a daily schedule or a to-do list to cover the next few days or weeks. Whatever works when you are not stressed will work now; it may just need to be exaggerated a bit to give you the same sense of security you were used to feeling.

Above all, I recommend that you avoid making any major life decisions at this time. Realize that right now you have got to focus on just doing what you need to do in order to get by. I often tell my therapy clients who are going through depression that negative emotions can cloud our judgment; as a result, we tend to make poor decisions for ourselves when we are not thinking clearly. The same applies for women who are experiencing miscarriage: our negative emotions and disappointment can make us do silly things, without even realizing it. Important decisions are best made when you are not depressed, stressed, or overwhelmed by physical or emotional pain. The most important thing now is for you to heal; everything else can wait until a later date.

This is also a time when you need to ignore any well-meaning friends who tell you not to worry at all or to push aside any feelings of fear. Your concerns and fears are perfectly normal, and you need to allow yourself to have them in order to address them and work through them. But that does not mean you have to let yourself be consumed by them. Unless your doctor has prescribed bed rest, staying busy with LIGHT activities—hobbies like cooking or knitting, or office work—will keep you engaged in your daily life, and that will ensure that you continue to move forward. If you are on bed rest, then read or watch movies. Now's a great time to rent those classic films you've been meaning to watch but never had the time to, or to read those novels that have been piling up on your bedside table. If you enjoy computer and video games, a game machine such as Nintendo or Play Station may also help the time pass and keep you active as well.

Your Partner's Needs

As I have emphasized above, you need to take care of yourself right now. But it is also important at this critical time to be very mindful of your partner or significant other. Include them in decisions if they want to be included, and make sure to sit down and discuss with them what level of involvement they are comfortable with. If you really need their support and they are not comfortable going with you for an ultrasound or for blood tests, you need to hear their reasoning before passing any judgment. They deserve your respect, too—different people simply handle things differently; that's all.

Maintaining your primary relationship during this stressful time is critical—who wants to endure the pain of losing both a baby and a primary relationship at the same time? And yet a miscarriage can cause all sorts of tensions within a relationship, and you must be prepared to handle them, too. The good news is that if you and your significant other make an effort to keep the lines of communication open, you should be able to reach a middle ground. The key is not to push them into anything they are uncomfortable with, while simultaneously making sure not to shut them out completely. Stay away from the extremes.

I'll say it again, because it bears repeating: the absolute golden key to getting through this period successfully is COMMUNICATION. Whether that entails communicating with your partner, your family, your friends, with your doctor or even yourself, it's all about making yourself clearly understood. This is already a confusing enough time in your life. The last thing you want to do is to add the doubt of a failing friendship, a strained relationship, or a misunderstanding with your health professional. If you don't understand something, ask. If you don't understand why someone is behaving in a certain way, speak up. Be respectful, but speak your mind.

I often get emails such as the following:

> *"This is my 3rd pregnancy in which we learned, prior to seeing any symptoms, that a miscarriage was imminent. I am now in the waiting process for things to start happening. Do you find this process easier or harder for those in this predicament? If asked to collect a tissue sample, how do others handle this? I am not even sure what to look for. What steps physically and emotionally do you suggest for starting over? How do I help my husband with this loss, as he is more concerned about me and doesn't talk about his needs or feelings of loss?"*

Remember, the key is to be open and honest—whether that means asking your doctor for clear answers in plain English or trying to get your hubby to talk about his feelings. Explain that you want some clarity and that communicating truthfully is the best way to enable the healing process to begin.

4

What to Do When You Get the Bad News

The First Hours

Some of the hardest words you will ever hear are the ones from your doctor, confirming that you have miscarried. I remember all too well what that experience was like. I felt a million feelings all at once. I wanted to run out of the room and hide! But unfortunately, I was in a doctor's office gown hooked up to an ultrasound machine with my legs in stirrups. It's hard to imagine a more vulnerable scenario than that. All I could do was to wait for the doctor to leave the room, redress, and then race to my car, where I could finally fall apart in private.

This is normal, and you should never feel ashamed for wanting to cry. You have lost a life that was part of you in a very intimate way. Chances are that you had already been dreaming of mothering this child, and now that hope has been dashed. This can be a very dark time, for everyone who has the misfortune to experience it. I totally understand how devastating it is when the excitement of early pregnancy turns to grief and loss.

On the one hand, getting the news at last can give you a sense of closure, putting an end to the excruciating waiting game. But although finally knowing ends the period of uncertainty, it also ends whatever hope you may have been harboring that this would all be a horrible mistake and that your baby would be fine. When you first lose this hope it can feel like having a limb torn from your body. It is enormously painful, almost too painful to bear! I know, because that is how it felt to me, and how it has felt to hundreds of other women who have shared their stories with me:

> *"My husband and I have been married for 9 years. We were trying for 7 years. I've been to 3 Reproductive Endocrinologists to help us conceive. I've had surgery (followed by infection). I've had 20+ IUI's (intra uterine insem-*

inations). I had 3 IVF's (in vitro). The 3rd IVF took place in September of 2004. My pg was fine. We heard the HB at 6 weeks and went WEEKLY for ultrasounds to the Fertility Dr. until 9 weeks. We then went to our OB at week10 and week 14. Both were fine.

"But at week 18 we went for our ultrasound and found out our baby had demised. There was no heartbeat. We were sent to a Neonatologist and had a D&E (yes D&E) performed 2 days later. I could go on about how emotionally horrifying this was—but I just wanted to share with you our story since it seems that you have been there and you care so much. Although miscarriage at any point is horrible, we can't help but feel that 'our' circumstance was beyond horrible. Our hopes were HIGH and came crashing down."

Given the enormity of this loss, you may want to take some time to live with it yourself before you start making the phone calls to your family and friends. This is your personal news, and you have every right to cope with it alone for now. Know that you don't need to tell everyone in your family right away. It is perfectly all right to take some time so that just you and your significant other can grieve your loss in private.

After you have had some time alone with your partner, you may want to start letting others know. It can be too painful to make the calls yourself, so I recommend asking either your partner or a close family member to make the calls for you, using a "phone tree" approach. To do this, ask everyone you or your significant other calls to call someone else on your list. This is really one of the best ways I have found to convey the bad news to those who love and care about you. Trust me, they will understand why you have not called them yourself. They all realize that repeating the news 12-15 times while calling all your family members is just not something that would be helpful to you right now!

You can always call them at a later time, when you are fully ready. Or, if you truly feel that telling your story now might ease your pain, then by all means call as many people as you can. As I will continue to remind you throughout this book, you and only you are in charge of your own healing. You always know what is best for you. You are the key ingredient to your healing, so always take the time to listen to your needs. The way you notify others about the miscarriage is an individual decision, and it is entirely up to you.

The Next Day

"At my routine 20 week ultrasound, we were supposed to be finding out the sex of our little bundle of joy. But instead we were told that he was dead. I was totally in denial until the doctor told me he was only measuring 17.5 weeks. I had an emergency DE&C done. Thank God that this doctor was one of only a few in PA that does this new procedure or I would have had to be induced. I just can't get over the fact that it has happened and truly need help, and so does my husband."

In moments of extreme stress, disbelief and confusion, many of us just need to find some facts and figures to hold onto. I know that for myself, my next inclination after hearing the news was to look to the Internet as a source of information. I was so confused about what was happening, and I felt the need to do research to edify myself.

But at this point I really want to caution you all to carefully qualify all information you get from the Internet. The Internet can be a fantastic source of knowledge, and a great way to find group support networks, but it is also full of misinformation and fraudulent predators. Before you put all your trust in a source, make sure it is legitimate. Before you believe a statistic or a health fact, check to make sure it is coming from a reputable source, not just from a person without professional training. This is another reason I wanted to write this book to make sure that a professional book was available to women so they could trust the contents of what they are reading.

You will probably find, like I did, that the Internet could be both very comforting and very scary. You will find some information that helps you, and other information that sets the alarms ringing in your brain. If what you are finding online starts to get overwhelming or makes you even more depressed, STOP! Step away from the screen! My husband actually took my computer to work with him for some time to keep me from becoming unduly stressed by what I was reading. I really thank him for that, because I know that if he hadn't, I would have become obsessed. If anything you are reading (including books) or looking at over the Internet is NOT helpful, put it aside for a while. You can always return to it later when you are feeling better.

Friends are another double-edged sword: they can be of great comfort, but they can also be full of horror stories at this strange time in your life. It is more than okay to tell people upfront how much information you can and can't handle. If you have a friend or relative who has experienced a miscarriage, it is also appropriate for you to choose not to reach out to them—even if those around you are pushing you to go to them for help. There will be time in the future to hear their stories—but only when you are ready to accept and listen to them fully.

Keep in mind that this is your time to take care of yourself. While it may be difficult, especially if you have other children at home to care for, just do the best you can. Adults around you will figure out how to help you, and children are very smart and sensitive. At certain ages they will be able to understand that Mommy needs some "alone time." You will probably find, as I did, that the people around you, from young ones to older ones, are on your side.

You may feel like a part of you has died, and it has, but know that you will make it through this terrible, empty time. One of my favorite sayings is, "This too shall pass." Give it some time.

Also, try to determine which aspects of your life you can control now, and which you cannot. Exercising control over that which you can control will give you some sense of stability, which is most important after losing something so dear to you—something that was actually a part of you. What aspects of your life do you have power over? Can you face going back to work right away? Should you hire a sitter? Do you want to be with friends or would you prefer being alone until the initial shock passes? Do what pleases you; you are the only one with the correct answers to these questions.

One thing that you cannot control, however, is your partner's response to this tragedy. Please remember that different people deal with their grief differently, and this is their right. Many men want to go back to work right away, as work is an effective "painkiller" for them. Allow them to deal with their pain in their own way, and try not to take it personally. At the same time, communicate to them what your needs are at this time, and make an effort to listen to them as they explain what they can and cannot give you.

> *"Just had my miscarriage last Monday. Felt very lost and angry too. Wanted to know what will happen to your body after D & C is done. How long will the discharge and cramps last? When can I resume my sexual life? Why does my husband take it more lightly than me???"*

Remember that what you want and need right now may be the exact opposite of what your significant other wants and needs. Men and women are so very different in so many ways, and response to stress is no exception. Be mindful and respectful of your partner's needs, and in return your partner will probably be better able to be mindful of your needs.

D&C vs. Natural Miscarriage

The first medical decision you will face after learning the news is whether to undergo a D& C to remove the remaining tissue or to wait until it passes naturally. This decision usually must be made while you are still experiencing a heavy sense of grief, and it can therefore be an especially difficult one to make. It is a highly individual decision, but your doctor and your partner can often help you to come to the choice that is right for you.

Your doctor can give you the pros and cons of each option—but in general, many women opt for the quick D&C, as it helps to quickly remove the physical pain and evidence of the failed pregnancy. Other women, however, feel emotionally unable to face such a sterile and unemotional medical procedure after their loss. They may want to undergo the natural process as a way of completing the failed pregnancy in a natural manner.

Whichever option you choose, make sure it is best for YOU and not just what your friends or relatives recommend. Always remember that it is your body, and you DO get a say in your care. Be aware that doctors will often recommend having the D&C done right away, so expect them to say this, and be prepared to ask for a little more time if that is what you want. Some women need a while to mourn their loss while their child is still inside them. In some cases that is okay, but in others it is not recommended. Again, your doctor will let you know if it is medically safe to wait just a little longer.

If you want to have the procedure done immediately, this is also perfectly normal. You may be completely uncomfortable with the thought of keeping your lost child inside you for any longer. If this is true for you, be sure to let your doctor know this. You can often have the procedure done the same day if you want to get it over with.

Remember that this is a procedure that you will need to take some time to recover from. Therefore, it makes sense to plan when you want to have it done based on the impact it will have on your life. Some women want to have the procedure performed on a Friday so that they have the weekend to recover. Others choose to do it during the week so that they will be healed by the weekend and able to spend Saturday and Sunday relaxing with their spouses and/or children.

"I found out yesterday that I had lost the baby. I had no symptoms of miscarriage. I had very light spotting after having intercourse. This was the reason I called the doctor. In two days I am going to go in to have a D&C done.

"Right now I think the hardest thing is that everything is still inside me. I have not expelled any of it. I was 12 weeks and 1 day along. I saw the heartbeat for the first time three weeks ago. It was so real then. I really could believe that I was pregnant.

"This was my first pregnancy. I am almost 28 years old and living with my boyfriend. It was a surprise for both of us since it wasn't in the plans. We accepted it and were getting more and more excited as my belly got bigger. I had gained 15 lbs by the 12th week. I was only sick twice and my only complaint about pregnancy was being tired and very emotional. The tired part had gone away in the past two weeks.

"But for some reason this last week I just had a bad feeling. Even though I have had no symptoms, I knew that something was wrong. It hurts a lot. Things happen for a reason."

Once you know that you have lost your baby and you begin preparing for the tissue to pass, you should be sure to educate yourself about what to expect. If you are unprepared, you will likely have a whole new round of stress, anxiety and terror when the process commences. Asking ahead of time will save you many phone calls and much worry later on.

Make certain that you know exactly how much bleeding and pain to expect, and what could indicate a problem. Doctors like to be technical, so ask your physician to be specific. If he or she tells you things like "excessive" pain or "large" clots, ask him or her to put it in a context that you can understand—clotting the size of "small oranges" or "8 maxi pads in 4 hours" worth of bleeding, for example.

It also helps to make out a list of questions to ask the doctors in advance and then write down the answers so that you can refer to them later on. Our memories are not good when going through this pain. A lot of us forget to ask questions at this time, because we are in a haze, or we find that the answers have slipped out of our minds. Writing down the information is something that your partner can help you with, and it can help him to feel more involved in the ordeal. Ask your significant other to bring the list of questions and write down the answers. This has two major benefits: it lets you both be involved and helps your significant other know what to expect. Later, therefore, your partner can help monitor you for any issues or complications.

> *"I found limited information about what to expect during the miscarriage. I searched, but found little about what I could expect to happen. How much bleeding? What would the level of pain be? Could I take pain medication now? How long would the miscarriage take? I felt like I was going through something completely blind. A week later I feel like I could of handled it easier if I'd known what to expect."*

What about the miscarriage itself? Well, you should expect to go through a great deal of physical discomfort and pain—I would compare it to a menstrual period times one million! Be sure that you have no strenuous activities scheduled, because you will not be able to do them. If you are unable or unwilling to cope with the discomfort, your doctor may be able to prescribe some pain medication, or you may opt to use over-the-counter solutions such as Midol or Ibuprofen. Be sure and ask your doctor ahead of time what medications are safe for you to use. Get lots of rest, and use a heating pad to help your insides feel better. You really don't want to start hemorrhaging at this time—so be sure to communicate this possibility to anyone who is watching over you.

Telling Other Children

At this time, you may also have the added burden of telling your other children. They were probably excited about the new baby—and now you must let them know that the baby is no longer going to join your family. It is important to convey this information in a way that they can understand, but without hurting or scaring them.

Before talking to your other children, therefore, be sure to take into account their developmental age. According to child development literature, children are not really able to comprehend death until after the age of seven. With young children, you will probably want to explain just a little bit of what happened, without going into too much detail. Just say, "The baby went to heaven," if you are religious, or "The baby is no longer with us."

Older children, however, will require more explanation. They may grieve in their own way, too. They may also be feeling some guilt if they had previously experienced any jealousy of the new baby. I suggest speaking with their school guidance counselor to get some suggestions about the best way to handle this, if you are uncertain. Sit your kids down and explain what happened in a straightforward manner. Be prepared to listen to their feelings and answer their questions as best you can. You may not have all of the answers, but your children will need you to at least talk with them and help eliminate their own confusion.

Above all, make sure not to ignore your children during this trying time. It is okay to tell them that you need some time alone before telling them what happened, but at least let them know that you will be talking with them at some point. Children, as stated earlier, are very quick to pick up on Mom's moods and will be wondering what is happening. If you don't say anything, they will worry about you.

> *"What is so hard sometimes is feeling that little Matthew won't be able to hold the little sister or brother I promised him. But he is well and I am grateful for that."*

Don't be surprised if your child doesn't show the signs of grief that you expected him to or that you feel are appropriate. As I have mentioned before, everyone grieves in his or her own way. It is possible that your child may not yet have experienced the baby as "real," especially when your child is under the age of seven. Remember that children may not yet understand fully where babies come from, and they may not realize, therefore, the degree of grief that is involved for the parents.

Handling Difficult Memories

If you miscarried at home, chances are that you saw some things that you would rather not remember, and that may be haunting you now. That is the case for this woman who wrote in to share her story:

> *"I was twelve weeks pregnant—my first pregnancy, at age 30. I started bleeding a little bit and I had cramps for three days. I did an ultrasound and the baby was fine. My doctor said that bleeding in an early pregnancy means you have 50% chances of losing it, but I had another ultrasound on Wednesday at 2 pm and it showed that the baby was OK. I was told that I had very good chances of keeping it. I was then instructed to stay in bed for a few weeks.*

"That night at around 10 pm, I felt like my water had broken. I called the hospital and they told me that at twelve weeks it is impossible to break my water. They said that since I had just had an ultrasound that same day there was no need to panic. A few minutes later, however, I had a contraction and a tiny three-months-old fetus came out in my bed. Then the placenta came out, just like a small delivery! At three months, the fetus is small but everything is there…. I looked at it as if it was my baby, with its cute hands and feet with tiny toes, etc….

"Then what do you do with the fetus? I could not get myself to throw it away as I sort of felt that it was my dead baby (anyway, whatever you do with a fetus at this point will sound creepy!). I once read that when you miscarry you are supposed to take whatever you can to the hospital, since in certain cases they will do an analysis which may help in determining the cause of the miscarriage. At least it will help the doctors know what, exactly, came out. So I took the fetus and the placenta in a plastic bag and took it to the hospital. They told me that they felt bad that they had misguided me when I called earlier, since it was really strange to break my waters and lose my child this way.

"What I did afterwards may have helped me. I came back from the hospital at 2 am, washed my sheets and cleaned up the blood everywhere, then put away all the pregnancy books I had in a closet. I then sent emails to everyone who knew I was pregnant, telling them that I had lost it. My husband initially thought it was weird for me to be writing emails four hours after the incident, but I felt that I would rather wake up the following morning without having to 'confront' everyone and tell them over the phone what happened.

"The next day I received sympathy emails and a few calls, and then I felt like it was behind me in a way. I think seeing the dead fetus is what traumatized me the most. I wish I had not had to see it! I also think miscarrying with a first pregnancy is the worst. Hoping I will get pregnant again soon-though I will unfortunately be so nervous the next time round!!!"

If your memories are particularly traumatic, I suggest you discuss them with a therapist or counselor to work through ways of minimizing their impact on you. There are several ways in which you can effectively deal with the images you saw of your unborn child.

One good technique for healing from this type of trauma is to picture the troubling event in your mind, then imagine it getting smaller and smaller until it fades away. This technique can be very useful if you are having nightmares about what you saw or have difficulty removing the scene from your mind. This technique is usually best learned in a therapist's office, so that you can control your reaction to the stressful picture, which may be quite traumatic for you.

A professional can help you with other methods for overcoming the trauma. Again, as these images can be very powerful and hurtful, it really is best for you to deal with them in a controlled, calming environment. I strongly recommend counseling for those of you who experience these recurring upsetting visions.

5

The Relevancy of the Five Stages of Death and Dying

When you lose a child you were carrying, even if it was only weeks into your pregnancy, you will experience the same feelings as if you lost a spouse or dear friend. Elizabeth Kubler-Ross, author of the much-acclaimed book *On Death and Dying*, left us a wonderful legacy when she described the five stages of grieving that we experience when confronting the death of a loved one. Those who have no personal experience with miscarriage often think that these stages only apply to the death of a family member or close friend. I know from experience that they also definitely apply to losing the baby you have been so eagerly anticipating and loving from the moment of conception (or even before, during those moments in which you dreamed about becoming a mother). In fact, it is often much harder to face the loss of an unborn baby, as you have no shared memories with this little person your body cherished and loved for so many weeks or months.

I believe it is important to understand the grieving process and to read up on literature about this subject. Why? Because that is a very good way to comprehend that your emotions are normal, and that everyone grieving the loss of an unborn child will experience these same emotions. Of course we all experience those emotions in slightly different ways, but we all experience them nonetheless.

I have often found, personally and in my professional life, that it can help tremendously in our healing process to be able to label where we are on the "map" of the five stages. For example, you may be able to think, "I am in my Anger stage now, and therefore I am healing." This is a powerful tool for moving yourself forward and on toward recovery.

However, I want you to know that these stages are not linear, which means you can cycle through and jump around these emotions many times before you are healed. You may be angry, then depressed, then angry again. Eventually, we need to move through all these stages to heal. When we keep cycling through the stages with no sign of advancing, it is a sign that our grieving may be unhealthy. It is also unhealthy to become stuck in one stage. If you have been in the anger stage for two years, for example, this may be a problem, and you might wish to see a counselor to help you move through it. But generally speaking, there is no set amount of time in which you must work through these stages. Only you can decide how long you need to grieve.

I went through each of these stages several times while I was trying to grieve my miscarriages. I know firsthand that it is especially hard to reach a point when you start to feel better, however, then you start to feel bad again—but this is normal. Try not to get too scared, worried, or frustrated as you experience these stages and cycle through them. Please know that what you are feeling is typical and part of the overall process of getting better.

The Five Stages of Healing

1) **Denial**—You may at first refuse to believe that you are not going to give birth to a live baby, or you may be in shock. It can be especially devastating if you have been trying for some time to have a baby. Some women turn to prayer, hoping that God will somehow make the doctor wrong or that a miracle will occur. This is perfectly normal; indeed, it can be a sign that even in the early hours of your grief you are beginning the healing process. You just want to close your eyes and have the day start over again—I know that is how I felt. I had been dreaming of my baby's first doctor's appointment when I learned that I had no baby and my world collapsed.

After your miscarriage, you will feel like you are in a fog; you may actually end up blocking out some of your memories from this time. This is very normal; so don't let it scare you. Even if your memories are blocked, just try to remember that this is your mind's way of protecting you from information that you are not ready to handle just yet. Don't ask too many questions if this is your situation, as it is just too soon for you to face things. You will remember what you need to remember when you need to remember it. And if you never remember, just let it go. Those memories are apparently too painful for you, and it is best that you not remember them after all.

"….I saw the fetus and I saw the heartbeat, but 5 minutes later…the movement stopped. They told me that I had to push the baby out myself and when that happened…I think I pushed my heart out too because I can't 'feel' anymore…I can't cope with this loss. I quit my job. I just want to sleep all the

time so I won't have to face reality. My heart exploded after the doctor told me what had happened…and my heart is still shattered."

It may not feel like it now—it may not feel like much of anything right now—but this stage will pass as time goes by. Trust me, it will. It may pass quickly or slowly, since different people experience the stages and the emotions in different ways. But eventually the reality of your loss will hit you (often like a ton of bricks) and you will begin to move onto another stage.

2) Anger—A lot of people get stuck in this stage, as it is a secondary emotion. It is always experienced when we are trying to block out a primary emotion that is just too painful to experience. Anger is someone's inner emotion turned outwardly to someone else. "How could this have happened to my baby?" "Why me?" "Why can I not have just one healthy child while many other women have several children and have never experienced a loss?" The anger stage can be directed at friends, family, at yourself, at your partner, or at fate in general. It can take many forms, and all of them are part of the grieving process.

The important thing at this stage is to let you be angry. Anger is healthy as long as it is dealt with in a healthy manner. I always tell my therapy clients that it is not their anger that worries me; it is how they deal with it that causes me to feel concern.

"….I was a devout Christian before this happened. Now I question God and I am angry at God. How come these stupid little thirteen year old girls get pregnant at the drop of a hat, drink, smoke, etc., and still have beautiful babies? It's not fair. It never will be fair.

"I thought about killing myself after it happened. I knew that my baby needed me and I am not needed here on earth now, so I wanted to die so I could be with my baby. There are so many things I will never know. I will never know if it was a boy or a girl, what color hair it had, what it could have grown up to be. But mostly I worry about my baby. It will never know how much I loved it. It will never get to be held in my arms. I experienced phantom limb type pain after my baby died. I never felt my baby inside me because it was too early, but now I feel like my arms should be holding a baby and yet I have no baby to hold. I have waited for this baby my whole life."

One of the essential things to realize at this point is that anger often masks other emotions. It could be covering up depression, guilt or other primary emotions. For example, if you are guilty because you miscarried due to an STD, you may be feeling intense anger at yourself. It is therefore crucial to deal with what you are feeling in a deep way, so that you get at the underlying emotion.

> *"Will the crying ever stop? What about this empty feeling? I know it was not my fault, but I cannot help but think that it was. I beat myself up all the time thinking about it, and now the only thing I want in the world is to be a mommy. I never knew how badly I wanted to be one until I lost my child. I am only 25 years old and I am afraid that it may happen again."*

One of the best ways to come to terms with your anger and its root cause is to keep an anger journal (see the journal at the end of this book for a guide.) Write about your anger: who is it directed at and why? Talk out loud about your anger, and write letters to whomever you are angry with—just DON'T mail them, of course! These exercises will help you to explore your feelings and better identify what it is that you are truly feeling deep inside. They may also help you to move through your anger stage. Most women are not comfortable feeling anger, especially when it is directed toward anyone else, and are anxious to move through this stage quickly. It is important to take this stage seriously and to confront our anger head-on.

When you handle your anger in this direct way, the underlying emotion will come out. If you can't get to it, however, professional help may be needed. You should never, ever feel ashamed of needing professional help, or of feeling angry. It is definitely okay to let this stage last as long as it needs to, just so long as it doesn't become unhealthy. If anger starts to interfere with your ability to be a good employee, wife, or mother, for example, seek help. Excessive unresolved anger CAN paralyze you, and that is when it becomes unhealthy.

One particularly common way in which our anger can come out after a miscarriage is in the form of "child envy." This is when you feel jealous of those around you who have healthy children. I know I certainly experienced my anger in this way, as have many others I have spoken with. This is completely normal, and it will pass with time.

> *"Now that I have lost the baby, I feel emotional all the time. When I'm with my friends who have children or are expecting, I feel jealous that it wasn't*

me, that I lost my chance. Even my boyfriend has a 4-year-old, so I cannot escape. I love my boyfriend's child but it's hard as he isn't mine."

For many months after I lost my first baby, I would stop and stare at children playing. I would have to choke back my bitter tears. I can't begin to tell you how painful it was, or how resentful I felt toward the parents of perfectly normal children—sometimes even my closest friends! What I can tell you is that what I felt is perfectly normal, and it's to be expected for quite some time.

If your feelings are too severe, I advise you to stay away from locations that have lots of children (parks, playgrounds, toy stores, etc.), and from friends who have children, until you are able to cope. If you believe that your friends will understand and will not judge you, you may want to explain your feelings to them. If you are worried that they will not understand your jealousy, simply keep it to yourself and find reasons to be too busy for a visit. Your feelings of envy will pass so just give it some time. I certainly don't recommend becoming a permanent recluse from all social events, but it is okay to limit your exposure to certain situations until your grief is manageable.

Some people find that it helps their grieving process to be around children, as it has the effect of making them feel hopeful about their own future babies. This, too, is okay. Just make sure you make the decision based on your own personal needs—and not the needs of anyone else. You do not need to share your feelings with those you envy, since they are not permanent by any means. They will start to dissipate soon, and you will probably find yourself back to normal when it comes to your friends and their families.

Two wonderful books that I recommend you read while working through anger are *When Anger Hurts* by Matthew McKay, and *The Dance of Anger* by Harriet Lerner.

3) Bargaining—Depending on your faith, you may find yourself bargaining with God or the fates or whomever you conceptualize as a Supreme Being. What do I mean by bargaining? "If only this news is a mistake, I promise to go to church every Sunday for the rest of my life." Or: "I promise to donate 10% of my income to charity." The specifics are as varied as the women who miscarry, but this stage of grief is practically universal. The tendency to bargain is totally normal. I personally remember thinking to myself, "If I am only allowed one healthy child, I won't ask for two."

This stage is the shortest of all the stages, but it can occur again at any time. It is important to acknowledge it, and then to move on.

4) Depression—This stage is the hardest one to get through and is the one that most women get stuck in. In fact, it is so important that I have dedicated the entire next chapter to a discussion of it. The stage of depression represents the upside of the grieving process, however. Depression is what we call a "primary emotion," so you should see it as a good sign. It indicates that you are moving forward in your grieving process.

It is perfectly fine to stay in this stage as long as you need to, but lingering in it for too long can be problematic if those around you don't understand your behavior. To help yourself out, I suggest that you keep a journal and write about your depression, just as you did when you were in the anger stage. Several main schools of psychological thought tell us that our thoughts lead to our feelings, which in turn lead to our behaviors. I will detail these in the next chapter on depression, but for now, all you need to know is that thinking can give you the power to change your actions. Start to identify the thoughts that create your sadness, and then challenge them. If you are thinking, "I will never have any children," changing this thought to, "I'd like to have children" can help you to start shifting your feelings away from sadness and toward hopefulness. Sometimes these thoughts can be automatic; you may not be consciously aware of them. This is why keeping the journal can really help you to bring them out.

Depression is often the hardest stage for our partners and spouses to understand. They usually feel that it should last an arbitrary period of time, after which point they begin to tell us, "Enough is enough." But if we are not healed by that unofficial deadline, it can create problems for us. If your spouse is exhibiting signs of frustration, try to translate it. What they are really saying is that they have exhausted all the ways that they know of to help you; they are frustrated. So try to open up and establish what you need and want in order to move on. As I have said before, good communication is very important in order to maintain your primary relationship while you are stuck in this fourth phase.

> *"I'm tremendously sad and depressed and my husband doesn't understand why I can't 'just shake it off.' He says it was nature's way, that it was for the best, etc. It would seem that since it wasn't a part of his body, he really wasn't attached to it. His body and mentality didn't go through all the changes mine did. I hope and pray that I can get through this. I know I can, but it would be helpful if I felt that he were a little more plugged in and that he cared a little more about how fragile and shattered I feel."*

Depression can be a healthy emotion, just like anger. But again, it is not the depression itself that concerns me when I am with my therapy clients; rather, it is how people act on their depression that is a subject of worry. We'll talk much more about this in the next chapter.

5) Acceptance—Finally, after we experience the pain and emotional anguish of the other four stages, we can arrive upon a place of peace: acceptance. Now what do we really mean by "acceptance"? I'm not saying that you aren't still sad and grieving over your loss. Acceptance just means that you have reached a place where you know that you can't change things; you must simply accept your situation and then proceed on with your life. It doesn't mean forgetting what happened, or even deciding that you are okay with what happened. What it does mean is that you are now able to function effectively as a wife, mother, or employee without getting sidetracked by your pain.

Once you have gained acceptance, you can again function in a healthy and effective way. You now have a strong sense of how to deal effectively with your grief. You need to know that you will never be the same person you were before—this is impossible to expect. This has happened to you, and you can't take it back. But you *can* choose to become a stronger, more confident person for having lived through this ordeal. In fact, many women develop a greater sense of purpose and meaning and become better friends, wives, partners, employees, and/or mothers because of this added depth of experience.

> *"I just want to let everyone know that by trying to reach out and help others I feel as though my baby girl's spirit has become a beacon for those also in pain."*

Now, you may start to realize that the sun will still come up, and the birds will still sing. You may not feel like looking at the sunshine or listening to the cheerful bird's song just yet, but you know that some day you will. This is the milestone we all hope to arrive at during our journey of grieving, but it may take us a while to get here. If it takes you a long time to reach it, don't worry. Everyone heals in her own time, and in her own way.

> *"I lost identical twin boys at twenty weeks gestation due to an incompetent cervix on October 28th. The cervix opened one night in my sleep and the next morning I delivered my still-born twins. My delivery was just like a normal vaginal delivery except my boys were not alive. Since this was my*

first pregnancy, I left the hospital completely empty-armed and absolutely devastated.

"My husband has been wonderful throughout this; in fact, it has actually strengthened our marriage. The one piece of advice I can give that has made the road to recovery easier is to absolutely live in the present, no matter how sad the present may be. Living in the past with all of its 'if onlys' and regrets, or living in the future and obsessing over another pregnancy, is not living at all. I have become more content and satisfied on this side of my tragedy by just focusing on this hour and this day, with all of its triumphs and trials."

6

Working Through Depression

Women and Depression

Depression is such a common phase among women who have experienced miscarriage that it deserves a chapter all to itself. In this stage, you may be so sad that you really don't know how to cope. It may be unlike any sadness you have ever experienced before or anything that anyone else you know has ever experienced before. Each experience is unique, so even if you have a friend or relative who has gone through a miscarriage, her experience will be different from yours. Depression is often the most paralyzing of emotions that can render even the strongest of women, weak.

> *"Last night, just as soon as the cloud of confusion began to clear and I could put my finger on a few of the things in particular that were making me feel sad, I voiced them to my spouse. People really do not know what it is that makes us feel sad. Those closest to us feel powerless because they can't seem to help us. I think we both felt closer after last night, when I was able to voice my fears, the sources of my sadness, and my continued attraction to him, despite my current lack of interest in acting on that attraction."*

Research shows that women experience depression twice as often as men, as we are more apt to turn our feelings inwards rather than outwards, as in the anger stage. We also know through research that depression is often the cause of missed workdays and poor job performance. Depression affects all aspects of our lives and is an emotion that is so tough to experience.

Depression is part of the grief process, though, which makes it an okay stage to be in, just so long as we have not crossed over the line into the danger zone. (In just a little bit I will give you guidelines for how to tell when to seek help.)

As a normal stage in the grieving process, it is important to accept your depression and work through it. If you fight against it and try not to be depressed, you might prolong your stay in this stage. However, you also don't need to feel like you need to stay in the depressed stage for any length of time if it is unnecessary.

The signs of depression vary from person to person—one person may gain weight and become lethargic, while another may become sleepless and lose weight. Any dramatic change in weight at this time can be a sign of depression. It may be difficult to tell since you have recently been pregnant, but you know your body better than anyone, so trust it to give you clues.

The Symptoms of Depression

The following is a list of symptoms that can help you to identify whether you are in a stage of depression. Check off the signs that apply to you:

- A persistent sad, anxious, or "empty" mood
- Feelings of pessimism
- Feelings of guilt, worthlessness, helplessness
- Decreased energy, fatigue, being "slowed down"
- Difficulty concentrating, remembering, making decisions
- Insomnia, early-morning awakening, or oversleeping
- Appetite and/or weight loss or overeating and weight gain
- Thoughts of death or suicide; suicide attempts
- Restlessness, irritability
- Persistent physical symptoms that do not respond to treatment, such as headaches, digestive disorders, and chronic pain

Seeking Help

I suggest that you take the time to rate your depression symptoms per the above list from one to five—a one meaning that you rarely experience this symptom, and a five meaning that you are never free of it—it is constantly with you. If you have three or more fives, or a consistent number of threes and fours, you may wish to seek professional help to get you through. At the very least, you may be able to identify how you experience your depression and target your coping skills accordingly. For example, if you experience persistent isolation as a result of your depression, then you may need to force yourself to spend more time with friends or family, if only for a short time.

At the same time as you are working through understanding your symptoms of depression, I also suggest you visit your primary care physician, as many symptoms of depression can actually be caused by medical conditions such as hypoglycemia or a thyroid condition. These factors may actually have been contributors to your miscarriage, so it is important to get some blood work done in order to find out and get treatment. For example, I was taught in graduate school that hypothyroidism can also look like depression in some people. Please get this checked out by your physician. You could save yourself more heartache.

One of the worst things that a well-meaning friend or relative can do is tell you to keep your chin up, or to keep saying that it will get better. This is usually the last thing a depressed person wants to hear, and it can actually wind up having the opposite effect. I advise staying away from those who want to give you free advice at this time, especially those who do not consider your feelings appropriately. This may mean ending phone conversations more quickly or leaving parties earlier than expected if you are surrounded by people whose words make you feel worse. Always remember that you are in charge of your own mental health—no one else. If someone is making you feel bad about yourself, stop spending time with that person-at least temporarily. As my mom used to say, "Kick me once, shame on you—kick me twice, shame on me."

Above all, if you are having recurring suicidal thoughts, take them seriously! Remember, if you act on these feelings, you will not be giving yourself a chance to heal or emerge from the grief and pain—nor will you be allowing yourself a chance to feel better or to become the mother you wish to become. You will not be able to continue being a mother to the children you may already have. Go seek counseling! The first thing a good therapist will ask you once you admit to suicidal thoughts is whether you have thought of specific plans or ways to carry out your suicidal fantasies. The counselor should then work on a no-suicide plan to keep you safe. Please take your suicidal thoughts seriously, if you have them. No one is a mind reader. You need to ask for help if this is your situation. Do not allow one tragedy to become two. Be honest and remember that you can and will feel better with some help.

"I go into my bathroom and lock the door to quietly cry, but I'm finding it harder to do so. I can be visiting with a close relative or a friend at church

and sometimes the smallest conversation can cause me to burst into tears. How can I gain more self control with the crying? My depression is becoming greater instead of better. My parents and my sister, who is an RN, feel I should have completely recovered emotionally from this by now. I am too ashamed to admit to them that I feel worse, not better."

Regardless of what you may think or what you may have heard, it is not a sign of weakness to need medication to overcome depression after your loss. Many women experience hormonal changes that create a chemically based depression, something that is best treated with medication. The medication will not work immediately, and you will need to take it faithfully for a period of time before you start to feel better. But when you do so, you will have the benefit of knowing that you are taking steps to take care of yourself and move yourself toward a more positive future if medication is necessary. Some primary care physicians are not comfortable prescribing medication for depression and may refer you to a psychiatrist. This is a doctor who specializes in treating mental health disorders with medication.

Types of Therapy

"I know from experience that you can't do it on your own. Find someone to listen to you—seek professional advice."

Through research, we now know that a combination of medication and talk therapy is often the most effective treatment for depression. There are many successful types of talk therapy, including Psychodynamic, Cognitive-Behavioral, and Rational-Emotive, to name just a few.

Both rational-emotive and cognitive therapists espouse the theory that thoughts lead to feelings, which then lead to behaviors. If you focus on your thoughts and write them down in a journal, you will learn to manage your feelings more effectively. Many thoughts are automatic and are ingrained in our subconscious—and thus they can be hard to grasp. But we can more easily uncover these thoughts through a combination of journaling and therapy, so that they can be reframed into something that is healthier and more valuable to us. Even if you don't opt for therapy, therefore, keep in mind that you can work to bring out the underlying causative thoughts through your practice of journaling. Writing things out can help you turn negative thoughts into positive, healthy ones.

Rational Emotive Behavior Therapy (REBT), was developed by Dr.Albert Ellis in 1955, and is based on the following ideas:

- You are responsible for your own emotions and actions;

- Your harmful emotions and dysfunctional behaviors are the product of your irrational thinking;

- You can learn more realistic views and, with practice, make them a part of you; and

- You'll experience a deeper acceptance of yourself and greater satisfaction in life by developing a reality-based perspective.

Rational-Emotive therapy can be very helpful as it causes you to focus on finding the solution within yourself, instead of expecting someone else to provide it. The basic premise here is that the only way we are able to heal fully is through our own efforts. Therefore, we must take charge of our recovery and healing process. An example of an irrational thought may be, "I need to be happy all of the time." This is not rational or reasonable. By identifying this thought, you can reframe (change) it to something like, "I enjoy being happy and strive for some happiness each day. However, some days are more difficult than others and that is ok."

Cognitive-Behavior Therapy combines two effective types of therapy—cognitive and behavior therapy—into one highly effective form of treatment. Behavior therapy helps you break your habitual reactions to problems that can be self-defeating. Cognitive therapy teaches you to change any thoughts that are giving you a distorted picture of reality, helping you reframe negative or depressive thoughts into healthy thoughts. For example, you may have a thought like, "I need to be loved by everyone." This could be changed to, "Not everyone is going to like me and I will still be a good person and like myself even if they don't."

Seeking out any of these types of therapies is a great way to cope with your depressed feelings. If you decide to seek professional help, it is okay and even healthy to interview therapists until you find one who feels safe to talk to and whose professional style of therapy is a good fit for you and your personality. As a therapist, I can tell you that we don't pretend to believe that we can be a good fit for everyone who walks through our doors. We know that some patients feel more at ease with us than others. So always remember that you are in control of your care—both with your medical doctor and with your counselor.

"I just recently had a miscarriage in August. My husband and I started trying again 1-2 days ago. To explain the emotions I am feeling is quite difficult...The pain and loss from our first pregnancy mixed with the excitement and prayers going thru trying to get pregnant are overwhelming. I am praying for the best. Before we started trying again, everything would remind me of the miscarriage—trying to understand, trying to find the reason for such a devastating experience. It is truly hard. With the help of loved ones, friends, family and co-workers, I have found some calmness, but still, nothing has ever made me understand WHY ME?"

Other Ways to Help Yourself through This Phase

In the last chapter, I discussed the many benefits of journaling to help you uncover thoughts and emotions that were keeping you stuck in one phase or another. While journaling, I suggest that you keep track of the times of day that you are feeling your best, as well as the times of day at which you are feeling your worst.

Now try and make sense of what is causing those bad times. What are your surroundings during your worst times? Do you feel your worst when you have to walk past the nursery at night before you go to bed? If so, you may want to ask your friends to help you convert the nursery back into a spare room. Is it when you are at work, near another pregnant woman? Once you learn to identify what your "triggers" are, you can work to find solutions for them.

On the other hand, consider what your circumstances are when you are at your best. Is this when you are cuddling with your partner? Then try to arrange time for more of this. Is it when you are with your friends or children? Plan to spend more time doing these activities, too.

Closure is an important part of moving on to the next stage, acceptance, and many women have been helped by having a funeral service for their child. You may even wish to name him or her to honor his or her memory. If this is impossible, you may consider writing down what you would say at such a funeral service, then placing the document in a revered place in your home.

"In Jan 2005, I am writing to support all women and their relatives. This is a death in the family. My daughter her partner and our families are grieving and it hurts. We can't have a funeral or some sort of ceremony, although

I wish we could. I am therefore planning to give my daughter a tree or some sort of memorial."

There also are a multitude of good books about depression on the market today. I suggest David Byrne's *Feeling Good* as one that can give you a great deal of practical suggestions for working through your depression.

The most important thing to remember is that the most effective help comes from within. Trying to make your spouse or partner responsible for your depression will place an unfair burden on him. It will only help temporarily, if at all. There are no magic words, books, or pills that will completely erase the pain of your miscarriage. If something doesn't work, move on to something else.

According to Freidrich Nietzsche, the father of Existentialism, in the end all friends and lovers are two ships sailing together in the night—and we must each act as the captain of our own ship. This means taking responsibility for our own healing, and taking charge of our healing process—no matter what others say or think. To ask someone else to be in charge of your life is not being fair to yourself. You can and will heal yourself in time and when you are ready. This will be the greatest gift you can give yourself-the knowledge and feeling of being able to take care of yourself.

Another thing to remember is that there is no quick fix for depression. Our society has taught us to expect instant miracle cures, like a yeast infection pill or antibiotics. But in this situation, you will not wake up one day and feel miraculously better. Instead, be realistic, and expect to feel a little bit less awful every day and then pretty soon, your less-awful feeling will change to kind-of happy and will then continue on to happiness; but all in good time.

Many people ask me why it is that they start to feel better and then something will happen and they will feel worse for a month, for example. They feel like this is a setback, but it is not. You need to remember that you started off feeling terrible all of the time and nothing made you feel better. Eventually, maybe even without your knowledge, you started to feel better. You are making progress, even with setbacks, and are better than when you first started your grieving process. Maybe now you feel good for a month and then bad for a month. However, soon enough, you will feel good for two months and bad for only one month, etc. This is how grief works. It is not easy, but you will get through it.

7

What If You Experience Anxiety Instead?

"At thirty-five, I just had my first pregnancy and miscarriage. I am now afraid that I may not ever be able to carry a baby to term. This fear coupled with the ordinary feelings of despair that accompanies miscarriage is debilitating."

As we are all different people, some of us will experience the fourth phase of grieving not as depression but rather as anxiety. This may sound like it does not make any sense, but sometimes people experience depression differently than expected. While most people experience depression as sadness, hopelessness, etc., some people actually have anxiety symptoms that are really depression. However, to make things more complicated, some people have true anxiety that is not depression. It is difficult to tell the difference and you may need to seek the help of a professional if you are struggling with high levels of depression, anxiety, or both. This can be a very difficult stage to pass through, as anxiety is so much of a physical reaction that it often feels uncontrollable. But it *is* controllable, as I will explain in this chapter.

Anxiety can be especially difficult for you to endure, since your friends, relatives and even your partner may not see that you need any assistance. They may actually see you being active and moving around and think it's a good thing! Sometimes anxiety means that you are on the go, constantly. You clean your house for hours, you exercise nonstop, or you shop constantly. These may not seem like problems, but they can be if they are done without an ability to stop or if they begin to interfere with your quality of life. Anxiety may seem less stressful than depression because you may not be showing the internal pain and stresses that you feel as much as you would be if you were depressed. However, anxiety can be just as damaging as depression.

Anxiety disorder can manifest itself as excessive worry about normal daily events—or even about having another child. In the extreme, it can manifest as panic attacks, which can be quite serious, but are treatable!

> *"I am finding it really hard to conceive after my 2 miscarriages. I feel less of a woman each day. I try not to obsess & stress about it but everything you do/eat you have to be careful as you MAY be pregnant. I want it soooooo much it hurts & I am sick of hearing 'it will happen when it's time.'"*

The Symptoms of Anxiety

- Restlessness, an inability to rest or relax
- Feelings of guilt, worthlessness, helplessness
- Being easily fatigued
- Irritability
- Muscle tension, unexplained aches and pains
- Difficulty concentrating due to a "racing mind," or mind going blank
- Difficulty falling or staying asleep, or restless, unsatisfying sleep

How to Tell If You Need Professional Help

As with depression, go through the list above and rate yourself on a scale of one to five for each symptom—one meaning that you don't experience it at all and five meaning you never have relief from it. Several fives or even fours and threes may indicate the need for help and should not be ignored. Even if you only have one five, you may need to seek help if it is severe enough to cause you not to be able to function in your life.

> *"Ever since my miscarriage, I have been having terrible problems with insomnia. I have been coping with medication but then feeling very guilty about it because I can't be on medication when pregnant."*

Specifically, if you find yourself getting dizzy, feeling overwhelmed, getting tight in the chest or—worse—having full-blown panic attacks, it is critical that you see a competent therapist and/or medical doctor immediately. Anxiety disorder is a painful condition that can be successfully treated in the majority of cases.

It can also be a symptom of a treatable medical condition such as lupus, hypertension, hypoglycemia, or a hyperactive thyroid. Some of these conditions also could be responsible for your miscarriage, so it pays to have some blood work done. If your primary care doctor is not willing to administer the appropriate tests, find one who will, since these tests are critical to your health and well being. Panic attacks can be life altering and need to be treated as soon as they arise. Panic attacks become worse the more you have them. They are a psychological disorder, but feel like a physical problem, like a heart attack.

There are several different types of anxiety disorders, such as social phobias, specific phobias, and obsessive-compulsive disorder, but they all fall under the main category of anxiety. As in the case of depression, remember that it is never a sign of weakness to need medication to control your anxiety. You have just experienced a very painful trauma in your life; taking care of yourself MUST be the first consideration. Also keep in mind that untreated anxiety disorder can ravage the body. When you experience anxiety, your body suppresses vital chemicals needed by your immune system—meaning that untreated anxiety may add further to your stress by leaving you open to any illness you are exposed to. If you can believe this, the doctors said that stress caused my first miscarriage. So, I know first-hand how damaging untreated anxiety can be. Do not let this happen to you.

Not dealing with your anxiety will trap you in a downward cycle. Anxiety can make you believe you are having a heart attack or brain aneurysm due to the intensity of the physical pain you can experience. It can also easily swing into a depression once your energy is depleted. This cycle can continue back and forth, confusing those around you and creating more inner turmoil for you as you work on healing. It's best to deal with it head on. Again, don't let this happen to you. Do not let your anxiety get out of control and lead to depression, missed time from work, or prolonged grief as a result of your miscarriage. Both depression and anxiety can cause you to stay in the grief cycle longer than necessary. If you are stuck in your grief, untreated anxiety or depression may be the cause.

How to Handle Anxiety

Mild to moderate anxiety can be easier than depression to self-treat as it is more of a physical reaction and less of a mental/emotional one. When you physically relax your body, it is impossible to remain in a state of anxiety. Therefore, I suggest that you visit a trained massage therapist or hypnotist and ask them to help you learn some relaxation techniques. As another option, guided meditation or progressive relaxation techniques are also quite helpful. Many guided relaxation tapes are available today in bookstores, and some directly address the need for restful sleep. Yoga is another option you may want to consider. The bottom line is this: if you learn to control your body, you will conquer anxiety. Think about it—if you are relaxing, you cannot be stressing and if you are stressing, you cannot be relaxing. To minimize your anxiety, you must learn to relax yourself physically and emotionally.

Again, as in the case of depression, journaling can help quite a bit when it comes to anxiety. As I mentioned earlier, you should note what times of the day you are at your best and worst. Try to draw correlations between how you feel and what is going on around you. This will enable you to identify your trigger points and to eliminate or lessen them.

Unfortunately, there is no quick fix. However, there are effective treatments. If you conscientiously practice your relaxation techniques and work to quiet your anxiety, you will find yourself feeling a little less anxious and panicky each and every day. There will be no dramatic overnight changes. However, that's a good thing, since small changes on a consistent basis are what you need at this point. Don't discount any positive progress that you see, no matter how tiny it may look.

A great book with many suggestions for handling anxiety is *The Anxiety and Phobia Workbook* by Edmund J Bourne. I recommend it highly!

> *"I suffered a miscarriage in December 2003 after a year and half of infertility. I became pregnant again in August of 2004 with triplets after fertility treatment. I lost one baby at seven weeks and then lost the twin at 16 weeks. I live every day fearing I might lose the last baby and wondering how I would cope with that. Every slight thing that might possibly go wrong makes me fear the worst. I am grateful for this baby that lives and cry for the ones I have lost. I am struggling to find peace."*

8

Coping with Guilt

After you have worked through your depression or anxiety, you may find that the underlying emotion that remains is guilt. Guilt can be fed by our own thoughts or by the careless remarks of others. It is a very difficult feeling to understand and overcome, and it is quite easy to become consumed with it if you are unable to forgive yourself for any real or imagined things you may have done to contribute to the miscarriage. Once again, I ask you not to beat yourself up too much—guilt can be a terrible emotion and very debilitating. Only when you are able to let go of your guilt will you become able to move forward with your healing process.

I know what this is like firsthand, because I experienced tremendous guilt. I worried about everything; from the sushi I ate to the amount of job stress I was experiencing. "What did I do to cause my miscarriages?" I kept wondering. Finally, however, I let go of my guilt. Once I did I felt much, much better.

> *"I didn't know I was actually pregnant until I started to have complications. I'm a vegetarian and have a certain amount of guilt that my diet contributed to my miscarriage. It has been nearly 2 months and I thought that I was OK until I heard about a comment that was made by one of my friends immediately after the fact. She asked my husband if she should forward information on vegetarian diets and miscarriages to me. I think he took it the same way I did and told her that it wouldn't be a good idea…"*

Often, the most effective way to deal with guilt is to do some research, aided by your doctor, into what actually caused the miscarriage. Usually, a miscarriage is due to a medical condition that is not your fault. Once you uncover the true cause, you may have an easier time releasing the guilt you have been harboring and begin to move forward.

It may help you to know that, according to medical studies, 50% of all miscarriages are due to the sperm and egg not fusing. Another small percentage of cases is due to a "blighted ovum," in which case the water bag and placenta (afterbirth) develop but not the fetus (baby). In 15% of miscarriages, a misshapen uterus is the cause of the problem; this condition is easily corrected with surgery. Other causes include a benign ovarian cyst, which is also easily corrected.

Ask your doctor to do some research to help you find the cause in your particular case, and then to correct the source of the problem so it doesn't happen again. The good news is that 90% of women who have miscarried once go on to have perfectly normal pregnancies in the future. Moreover, the vast majority of miscarriages happen through no fault of the mother's. Keep telling yourself this; it can help to lessen your guilt. There is nothing you did to cause this miscarriage and you are most likely able to have healthy children.

If you do find that the cause was an STD or something you did contribute to, acknowledge it and then start to try to forgive yourself. None of us are perfect, and we all do things that we regret later on. It is only human nature. In order to release yourself from guilt, try writing a letter to yourself or to your child. Tell yourself or your child how very sorry you are, expressing all the feelings you have kept inside. If you take this action, you may find that it greatly alleviates your guilt by giving you a way to actually rectify the situation in some small part. Even if you are not sure about this idea, try it anyway. You may surprise yourself at how freeing it is to write on paper your thoughts and to get them out. We are often held hostage by our emotions bottled up inside and one of the most healing things you can do is to let your emotions and thoughts out. You can do this by talking with friends or family, by writing a letter (not to be sent) or by talking with a therapist.

"My name is Melissa and I have suffered through 3 miscarriages. More than that, however, I wanted to tell my story for another reason. After the first miscarriage I was in shock—none of the women in my family had ever had one, and I had never dealt with this.

"One of my family members told me to take this pill that had helped other women who had miscarriages, so I did. I am young and I did not think twice about taking the herbal pill. Then I went on to have two more miscarriages, really similar to each other. So I went to the doctor to have a test because I was sure that there was something wrong with me.

"All the tests turned out fine, so I asked her about the pill I was taking. I had asked her after the first miscarriage if it was ok to take it, and she had said

that she did not think it would help me stay pregnant but that it would not hurt me, either. So after the third miscarriage, when I asked her again about the pill, she checked in the big book and said it was very dangerous in pregnancy.

"So I just really want to say that you should never take anything you're not sure of. Always check everything out very well and MAKE the doctor look it up for you. I thought I was helping myself when I could have been hurting myself. I want to make it clear that I am not sure that this caused my miscarriages, but if I had done more research on it I might not be writing this today. So it is something to watch out for. I take full responsibility for taking the pill—I just don't want anyone else to do this same thing."

If this miscarriage opened your eyes to a medical problem that you were not aware of before, then tell your child in the letter that his or her life was sacrificed to save the lives of his or her future siblings. Tell him or her how much he was loved, and that you are sorry that you didn't know about the issue in time. If this idea of sacrifice does not give you peace, then keep searching for another idea that can give you peace. You will be able to make sense of what happened—it just takes time. Make sure you give yourself the time.

Sometimes the guilt you feel may be partly due to your having mixed feelings about the child you were carrying, too. This can especially be true if you were in a bad relationship, or if you were not in a traditional relationship. I have talked with many women who did not actually plan on becoming pregnant and were not sure they even wanted a child. However, most women say that they became used to the idea of being pregnant and some even became excited about the idea. However, when they miscarried, these women suffered extreme amounts of guilt over having ever doubted whether they wanted the child and whether their uncertainty caused the miscarriage. Always remember if this is your situation, the child did not know the circumstances under which he or she was conceived. They did not fail to survive because of any mixed emotions on your part. You must learn to forgive yourself if this is your situation. Maybe you can even learn something from this experience-like the fact that maybe you do really want a child. Whatever you can take with you in terms of internal growth as a person can help make this miscarriage less of a tragedy. Make something positive come from this loss. If you are not able to do this now, you will be able to soon. Hang in there.

"I am writing as a woman who is not in a traditional relationship. I had a miscarriage, and I know my personal struggle has included feelings of relief seeing as how now I don't have to raise a child with a man I do not love, as well as not having the guilt of an abortion. I do, however, have HUGE feelings of guilt regarding the simultaneous relief and loss I'm feeling."

These mixed feelings are often present in the very young, who worry that they may not yet be ready for the responsibility of a child. All your feelings are a part of you, and they are natural and okay. Give yourself permission to feel them. You need to accept them, then forgive yourself for them. None of us has walked in your shoes and now is not the time to let anyone guilt you about your life choices. One of the reasons people find therapy so helpful is that a counselor is someone in your life who is not going to judge you for what you have done, or thought, or felt. You NEED someone in your life like this—someone who will let you be you, without justification. Find that person, even if it is a counselor.

Forgiveness is a difficult yet necessary step in healing. Think about other times in your life you have had to forgive. What did you do to get to the point where you could handle this? What does forgiveness mean to you? Does it have a religious basis for you? Forgiveness is such a personal matter and one that you will have to find out how to achieve for yourself.

If you are a religious person and view forgiveness from this perspective, it may be healing for you to speak to a pastor or religious leader about your feelings and struggles. It also may be helpful for you to talk to others who have had to forgive things in their lives. It doesn't have to be the same type of forgiveness—someone who has had to forgive an alcoholic parent will also have some wisdom to share. The core of forgiveness is the same, no matter the issue that generated the need for it in the first place.

The philosophy of Existentialism tells us that there is a higher meaning for every event in our lives. Nothing happens without a reason. It can therefore be very useful to discover the meaning that this event will have for your life. Everyone will turn up a different meaning, as no two of us are alike; but the moral here is that we can all find a meaning if we search hard enough for it. Finding the meaning this miscarriage can have in your life can be freeing. Trust me, I know. I used this miscarriage as a sign to work on some of my own issues that may have prevented me from being the best parent I could. I took my miscarriages as a sign to strengthen my marriage to provide the best environment for a child. I still struggle from time to time with why these miscarriages had to happen to me, but

I am also pleased with the work I did on myself. I was able to turn something terrible into something positive.

For example, my husband and I took our tragedies as an opportunity to make things right in our lives. We used our losses to build our relationship and grow as a couple. We found that we were not really communicating as well as we should to become good parents. We are now better people and better partners to each other because of the pain we shared. Without these shared anguished experiences, the need for us to improve would not have been apparent.

9

Advice for Partners and Significant Others

If you have a wife or partner who has just experienced a miscarriage, you have the opportunity to be either a tremendous source of help and support or to inadvertently add to her pain. This chapter is devoted to helping you, the partner or friend, understand how to help her through this trying time. It's also intended to help you become a better partner over all.

The first concept to remember is that you have no idea of what your partner is going through physically. So do not minimize her pain or tell her, "It's not so bad." It is not helpful to act like this experience is something you have been through or to imply that you have firsthand knowledge of it. You are not going to be able to relate to it either physically or mentally, so don't attempt to. That will only make her feel like you are minimizing her pain and distress. Even if you have experienced physical suffering before, please do not start to compare your pain to your partner's—she will not be relieved by the comparison. You need to let her tell you what it feels like and believe her. This is the most intense pain I have ever experienced—and I have had my ear bitten off by a dog!!!

Of course, one of the best things you can do is to educate yourself about what your partner is going through right now. Even the women who undergo miscarriages can be quite confused about the experience, so no wonder most men are mystified.

> *"I miscarried 2 days ago after a four-day process of extremely heavy bleeding and severe cramping just before I passed cleanly a ten-week-old fetus. I was told to take a day or two of bed rest, and then the bleeding would stop and cramping would go away. Well, right before I actually passed it, suddenly my abdomen got like twice the size it was, and when I would drink water or eat anything, almost instantly I would get a bulge in my stomach and feel*

like I was peeing but it was blood instead. When I called up the ER and told them what I was feeling, they said not to drink any water…

"Well, it's been two days and I'm still very noticeably bloated and distended in my whole belly. I'm still experiencing constant cramping, mostly in my back and upper stomach, like a fist tightening. I get dizzy every time I move. I am still bleeding and shedding tissue clumps if I do anything at all. I've hardly had anything to drink or eat because I feel like I'm gonna pop.…Could I be bleeding internally and that's why this uncomfortably bloated stomach won't go away? It's the weekend and I'm not getting any return calls from my doctor.…"

The cramps the woman is describing here are very similar to labor pains—and you're probably very aware of how excruciating that entire process can be. Whether your partner miscarries naturally or chooses to have a D &C, know that it is going to be enormously painful. One of the most important things for you to do during this period of time is to monitor her carefully for any signs of complications. Ask the doctor what level of pain, bleeding and clotting is normal, and make sure that you notify the doctor if you see symptoms that are outside of these guidelines. Write down all the information the doctor gives you in detail.

Along those same lines, you can help your partner a great deal by taking charge of the communications with the doctor. Make a list of questions for the doctor before your next visit, and make sure you write down the answers. What and how much medication should your partner take? How often? When should she come back? What are indications of complications? Your partner may be in a daze later on and not able to think logically about what questions to ask. You should be prepared and step in for her in her time of need.

She will probably want to go straight home from the doctor's office and may be on bed rest for some time. As she will not be able to drive, you will most likely need to stock up on supplies such as maxi pads, movies, books, medicine, and magazines for her. People will need to be notified about the end of the pregnancy, so you can also be proactive by setting up a phone tree and making the initial calls until she is ready to talk to others. To do this, make a few phone calls and ask each person you talk to—to call a few other people. This way you can notify everyone who needs to be notified in an efficient manner.

Before you make those calls, however, it will be important to find out how comfortable she is having others know about what happened, and how much she wants them to know. Be sure to respect her wishes. Don't just think that she won't find out—she will.

At the beginning of the process, it is a good idea to ask your partner how much alone time she wants and how much she wants your company. Respect her wishes. If she wants to be alone, give her some space; but if she needs more of your time, try to clear your schedule to give it to her. Miscarriage can be a tragedy, but it can also be a chance for the two of you to bond more closely, as she will not be able to do much but rest. Games and movies may be excellent ways to cheer her up during her recuperation. But if she is not interested in either, don't push it. Instead, try to figure out what she wants to do. Does she want to play video games? Bring in a Nintendo and set it up by her bed. Does she want to read books? Bring her a stack of her favorites. Do not use your down time from work as a time to have friends over, unless that is what she wants. This time off from work is not a vacation for her. Try to come home for lunch or call often during the day, if you cannot take a few days off from work.

> *"How do I make my husband understand that while he is hurt, I feel like it is really only my hurt? I know others, my mom, dad, and husband hurt for me..."*

This is a time when your partner is not going to be able to contribute much around the house. You should therefore be prepared to take on more household responsibility than you usually do. If your work schedule doesn't permit this, then arrange for her to have help. Relatives can be very handy now, and they may be eager to step in and help during this trying time for both of you. If you don't have any relatives living nearby, considering hiring a cleaning or personal care service temporarily.

Assume that this is the beginning of an uncertain future. Different people heal differently and at different rates of speed. You have no idea of what she is going to go through, so be careful not to set expectations as to any timing for her recovery. Each woman handles pain differently. Ask her what you can do to help, but know that it is primarily her responsibility to heal her own emotional distress at her pace and in her own way.

This also means that what might be helpful to you may not be helpful to her. Pushing her to go back to work if she is not yet ready may not help her, even if it was the most healing thing for you. Women typically need to take more time to stop and take stock of their lives than men do. Respect this difference and give her the support she needs, regardless of her decision.

And what about attempting another pregnancy? Well, if she is not ready to try again, the worst thing you can do is to push her. Both of you must be ready to try again in order for it to be a success—having a child is a joint decision, after all. Likewise, if she holds out hope for a future child, now is not the time to crush her hopes if you feel otherwise. Postpone this discussion until she is better able to participate fully; she needs time to heal before making a life-altering decision. Remember, too, that you are still grieving as well. You may very well change your mind later on.

As I have mentioned, everyone grieves in different ways. Your partner may exhibit some personality changes during this period that could cause you some alarm. For example, her normally extraverted personality may turn introverted, or she may become pessimistic when she was a true optimist before. This is not a cause for concern and is usually only a temporary response.

> *"…Thank God for my husband! He is strong but sometimes I would like him to show his emotions. At times it doesn't seem like it affects him like it does me."*

You will also be going through a time of intense pain—and it is not wise to bury your feelings and deny your need for healing. More than women, men tend to keep their feelings bottled up, and this can be very damaging to you emotionally and physically. It's okay to admit to your grief. It isn't just your partner who is experiencing pain, so try to take some time to sort through your feelings, too. Reach out to friends and family, and see a counselor if you find your emotions overwhelming.

> *"Why is it that you can get up to twenty weeks and still suffer a miscarriage? I went to work happy that morning—it had actually been a strenuous weekend and we had had a day off Monday to have a scan done. No problems. Heartbeat fine, doctor was happy.*
>
> *"Tuesday I go to work and my wife calls me at about 10.30 am. She tells me the bad news and I am in total disbelief. I get to the hospital thinking it's a mistake, and we have another scan in the afternoon. It's then confirmed right before my eyes. Why? How? I thought at first, was their scanning equipment calibrated, was it working okay?*

"I am beside myself. I can't talk to baby because baby isn't there anymore. Tomorrow my wife has to deliver. But she is facing up to so much. I can't sleep, she can't either. She even told me she had had a dream last year to say that baby would die. How does this help me?"

Above all, remember that you are both there for each other. Reach out for each other and provide the comfort that only you can give at this most difficult of times. Don't forget to take care of yourself during this process because your partner may not be able to care for you for awhile—she is barely able to care for herself.

10

Insensitive Comments: How to Handle Them, and How Not to Make Them (A Guide for Friends and Family)

"I wonder about how to deal with people's comments that just don't help—i.e. 'It was for the best,' etc.?"

"I am a licensed mental health therapist and have just miscarried at 10 weeks. I think the worst part was dealing with the awkward responses of others."

At this time in your life, you will be feeling much more vulnerable, sensitive and emotional than usual. This makes sense from a physiological standpoint: our minds filter information differently when we are grieving than when we are not. Unfortunately, this is the time when many will make comments that hurt you. Just realize that those comments come more from ignorance than from any malicious intent. Though they can really hurt sometimes, even intensifying the depression, anxiety, or guilt you are already feeling if you are not prepared for them, they are generally not intended to have this effect.

"How do you make the people around you understand you can't just forget and that it is a big deal?"

Preparing you for the inevitable responses means being proactive. Before you make the announcement, decide who needs to know about what has happened, and then decide how much of the details about your miscarriage you want them to know. What is your comfort level with others at this stage? Are you prepared to discuss the specifics with people if they call? Remember, you are in charge when it comes to this highly personal event that has just taken place in your life. It is up to you whether you let others discuss it with you, or if you keep it mostly to yourself for now.

When you do receive an insensitive comment from someone you care about, do not react with anger, even if that is your first inclination. Instead, take a deep breath and say, "Your comment tells me that you really don't understand what happened to me. Would you like me to explain it to you?" Assume that your friend or relative cares enough to have said something at all; they just really don't know how much their comment hurt you. So get rid of that comment! Visualize the trash bin of your computer, put their comment into it, and then click "empty"!

Often, it is just a waste of breath to try and explain to them why their comment was insensitive. It is often better to just ask them, "Would you like to know what to say that would be helpful?" If you treat others with this level of patience and grace, the comment they made to you may be the last insensitive thing they ever say to a woman who has recently miscarried—and you can be sure you are not the last person they will come in contact with who has miscarried.

Being able to respond with maturity during your time of pain will not be easy, and it will take some practice. To prepare for it, role-play situations with your significant other or your friends before you encounter an actual situation like the ones described above. Being prepared will make it easier for you to respond in such a way that you do not alienate a long-term friend. It will also make you feel better about your responses.

> *"I have now had three miscarriages and one healthy baby boy. Everyone seems to think that the two miscarriages I had before my son are somehow 'ok' because I have a baby. I had my last miscarriage Christmas Eve this year, and I am sick of hearing, 'Oh well, at least you have Michael (my son).' How can I stop feeling so angry and upset?"*

Remember that people may just be mirroring comments that they have heard others say, or that were said to them if they have had a miscarriage. These responses, unfortunately, have a long history. I call them "stock comments"—they are like stock responses or clichés.

You may also receive insensitive comments from medical staff or even your own doctor. If this happens, try to keep in mind that these professionals have to deal with death on a daily basis—if they didn't become somewhat desensitized, they would go crazy. Again, just let these comments go. Imagine your computer trash bin, and get rid of them.

> *"I'm a clinical social worker and recently lost a baby. I was really shocked by the insensitivity of the medical staff and providers."*

If you find the medical staff so uncaring that it offends you, remember that you always have the ability and right to change doctors. There are many doctors available in most areas, and you are sure to find another good one if you look hard enough. It is important to have a physician that will treat you with respect and the appropriate level of sensitivity. Respect is very important at this stage of your healing.

If you receive an insensitive comment from someone you know to be a genuinely insensitive person, don't even waste your time trying to explain anything. Just remove yourself from the situation immediately—excuse yourself to go to the restroom, or do whatever you have to do to get yourself out of this person's presence. Compose yourself, and try to stay away from this person until you are ready to handle them. People like this are all around us, but they really don't deserve our time and attention. If you allow them to upset you, you are giving them more power than they merit.

How To Communicate With Someone You Care About Who Has Recently Miscarried

> *"One of my brother's closest friends just had a miscarriage. She was 3 months pregnant and I am 2 months pregnant. I feel really terrible for her and was looking for some decent, sensitive things to say to her."*

This is a tremendously difficult time for your friend or family member—she has lost a large part of herself and badly needs your understanding and support, even if she may not be aware of it yet. You can do a lot to help her, even if you don't see how at this time. Many women who have healed from this trauma attribute it all to their caring and loving family members and the friends who saw them through.

The most important thing to remember is to THINK before you say anything. If you don't know what to say initially, it is better to be quiet for a while than to say anything that could potentially be construed as hurtful. Don't be quiet for too long, however, as she may take it as a sign that you don't understand or don't care. This can be a difficult balance to achieve, so take your cues from her. Feel free to say to her, "I don't know what to say, but how can I help?"

"…It's even harder when your family and friends don't understand and say insensitive comments!!! You never get over it but somehow you try to get by. It's very hard! I try to keep faith!"

Here is a guide to some of the common phrases I and other women have heard, but that you definitely do NOT want to say to someone who has miscarried:

- "At least you have other healthy children."
- "It was meant to be this way…."
- "The child would have been born defective/deformed/sickly anyway."
- "You must have done something wrong…."
- "Did you take your prenatal vitamins?"
- "Don't worry about it, it will be okay."
- "You can always adopt or try again."

The last comment is something you may say later, when she has had more time to process her pain, but it is not going to be very helpful in the early days following the miscarriage.

"…And I love how everyone tells you not to worry about it—how can you not?"

Here are some things you can say that ARE helpful:

- "I am sorry for your loss."
- "I am very sad for you."
- "Is there anything I can do to help?"
- "I can't imagine what you must be going through. Is there anything I can do to help?"

Above all, don't assume you can relate to her pain, even if you have experienced a miscarriage. Again, every woman is different. And if you cannot offer genuine empathy, just offer her your support and be a good listener. Ask her to share her experience with you, if she wants to.

> *"I have a very close friend, Jen, who suffered a miscarriage today and I would like to give her any information that might help to get her through this very sad time."*

Be aware that a woman who has just miscarried may initially push you and her other close friends and relatives away. If she does, make sure that she knows that you are there for her. Don't take her initial response as a flat-out rejection. There will come a time when she is ready to accept your help, and if you quit extending your helping hand when she is ready to reach for it, it will be a sad thing. She will let you know when she needs you. In the meantime, just knowing that you are there for her will be helpful.

11

Your Future Choices

Trying Again

"This is a big loss. I do look to tomorrow with the hope and faith that our next pregnancy will result in the beautiful children God intends us to have."

Right now, as you are reading this, the future may seem very uncertain to you. Will you try again? Should you try again? How will you know when you are ready? Will you ever be ready? Will your partner ever be ready?

There are two events that have to happen before you are truly ready to attempt another pregnancy. One, you have to be physically whole; and two; you have to be through your grieving process and emotionally whole. Rarely do these two events happen at the same time, however. Most of the time, one will occur first, and then you will have to wait for the other.

"My husband and I are thinking about trying again straight away after I stop bleeding, as I have read a pregnancy magazine that states that there is no harm at all in doing this and that it may actually benefit the pregnancy because my body has just had a trial run. I just wondered what your thoughts on this were."

Doctors usually advise waiting three months before trying again, as your uterus and cervix need to return to their pre-pregnancy levels. Your hormones also have to adjust—if you get pregnant again before this happens, it will be impossible to date your pregnancy. This can create difficulties and add to the anxiety you will already be experiencing with your next pregnancy.

"I too am a clinical psychologist and am having great difficulty coping with my recent miscarriage. Any advice on trying to conceive again after such a big loss?"

I recommend consulting your doctor, as other factors may make it prudent to wait longer than three months. You may want to find out what the problem was and fix it so that you don't have to endure another miscarriage. It will take time to find the root cause of your miscarriage, if it is indeed possible to uncover it at all. If your doctor is not giving you answers or refuses to dig more deeply into the cause, don't be afraid to change doctors. Don't ever worry about hurting doctors' feelings—they are there to help *you*. If they aren't, then find someone who will give you the help and support you require.

Most insurance companies will make you wait for three months before running tests—but you can self-finance if you have the resources to do so. Some ob/gyn doctors can run tests themselves so that you don't have to go to an infertility expert. The cause could be something as simple as a misshapen uterus that can be easily fixed. It would be a great shame not to know about such a cause, because correcting it can make it much likelier for you to conceive and carry a healthy baby to term.

But of course it is not enough to be physically ready; you also have to be mentally and emotionally ready. It is rare that you will be both physically and emotionally ready at the same time—in fact, you will probably have to wait for one or the other conditions to catch up. The worst thing you can do is to get pregnant again before you have fully grieved your miscarriage, although some women are tempted to do this in order to erase the memory of the pain. Does it help? Absolutely. But this is the wrong reason to get pregnant. You will still have residual feelings to resolve after you have delivered. These feelings can interfere with your ability to parent your new child or even to handle another miscarriage should it happen again.

How will you know when you are ready? When you are able to function effectively without having the pain interfere with your ability to perform as a wife, mother, or worker, you will be ready. You will know when you reach this stage. You will not have forgotten—you can never forget—but you will be able to cope.

It is also critical to understand that it is rare for both you and your partner to be ready at the same time following a miscarriage. It is truly unfortunate when one of you decides to never try again and one of you desperately wants a child! This situation calls for open and careful communication, performed with love and gentleness.

What to Do if Your Partner Is In a Different Place

"How does a person who has four kids already but wants another decide to have another when their husband is done? He also doesn't want me to go through another miscarriage. I have had three. I had my fourth child after the first miscarriage and before the second two. The emotional side of me doesn't want to quit."

If your partner is at a different point than you are, it is very important to communicate. Listen to your significant other's reasons for not being ready, or for wanting to get on with it! Make sure that you each listen to each other and know what the other one has gone through or is still going through. Talk out your hopes, fears, and dreams—you may even find that it brings you closer together than you were before. It is possible that your partner experienced more grief than he showed at the time, and that he needs more time to heal. It is also possible that your partner sacrificed his own healing in order to help you through. It is important to talk all of these things out honestly and openly before you make decisions about your joint future.

Trying again must be a mutual decision—neither one of you should push the other into another pregnancy if both of you are not ready. That could be disastrous to your marriage, even affecting your child and his or her future happiness. Children can sense any dissonance in their parents, often from a very early age.

"Initially, Derek said that we could try again, and I therefore considered the loss temporary. One month later, however, Derek announced that he didn't want any more children and that he would not try again….then the grief hit me."

If in the aftermath of a miscarriage you discover that your partner is not the right person for you, you may have to grieve both losses. It is very easy to be nice when things are going well, but the true character of a person comes out when things are not going well. If your partner or mate has "stopped being wonderful," you have to ask yourself what kind of parent they would make, or if they are really the person you want to have children with. It is hard enough for children to grow up in this world with two good role models, so how would your kids handle it if one of you didn't end up being a good role model? Studies have proven that it is not divorce that damages children; it is being subjected to constant battles between their parents that creates the most harm.

"I had a miscarriage yesterday. I thought I was pregnant—I just knew it. But due to stress I lost it, and I remember exactly when it happened. I'm not like most women. I wasn't far along, but this is something I wanted. Although I am engaged he got "spooked," in his words, and I went through it alone. It is now New Year's Eve and all I can think about is that in the year 2005 I was gonna have a baby. My fiancé did say it's probably for the best. It hurts and I feel alone. I just thought I would say if you had a miscarriage and you have a guy that will stand by your side and help you through it, think positive; you will probably get pregnant again. Well, my New Year's resolution is to think positive, because who knows, I may find a guy who will be there if it happens again."

If You Choose Not To Try Again

After you work through your pain and loss, you may find the thought of holding an adoptive baby comforting and warming. This option may help you feel secure in the knowledge that you will never have to go through a miscarriage again. You can also be happy knowing that you are giving a child a chance in this life that he or she may not otherwise have had. Many adoptive parents feel good about their decision for this reason. Remember, it takes more than just biology to make someone a parent! A magical thing happens when a mother cares for a baby—both the baby and the mother bond as though she had given birth to the child herself.

If you choose to go this route, be sure to check out the adoption agency thoroughly before you engage with them. There are many less than reputable agencies out there that can cause you a different sort of pain altogether.

"The areas that concern me most are how to make the decision to not try again and how to react to a society that feels a woman isn't whole without babies."

Also, many people end up finding peace with their decisions not to have children once they miscarry. This is always an option, and it's perfectly appropriate to consider it. You are not a failure if you decide not to try again. Only you can decide your next course of action following a miscarriage. Many women are childless, and they find enormous fulfillment in their careers, marriages, family, and hobbies. Perhaps the best choice for you is to devote your time to another path entirely—but remember this is YOUR choice and no one else's.

Handling Anxiety When Trying Again

When and if you do decide to try again, anxiety over what will happen this time is completely normal. I went through it, and yes, I had yet another miscarriage. I share that with you not to alarm you but rather to be honest about my experiences.

In reality, it is much more uncommon to have two miscarriages than to have one. A majority of women who endure a miscarriage will only have to experience one in their lifetime. However, there are some of us who have to experience multiple miscarriages before having a healthy child. There are also many women who have healthy children, miscarry once or multiple times, and then go on to have more healthy children. Again, there is no rhyme or reason to miscarriages most of the time, and I cannot begin to explain why so many of us have to experience these losses. But the reality is that we do.

> *"The thought of going through this all over again is very daunting. There are no answers right now and this is tough…."*

If you experience undue anxiety when trying again, reread my chapter on anxiety and follow some of the suggestions I have provided you with. Also, keep the facts behind miscarriage firmly in your mind. When you start to think irrationally and fear the worst, remember the statistics and allow the probabilities to comfort you. Your partner or significant other can be a great source of support during this time, especially when you both know the odds and realize that they are in your favor.

12

Some Parting Words

I sincerely hope that this book has provided you with some comfort and solace, and that it has also helped you deal with some of the practical aspects of your situation.

If there is one thing you take away from this book, please remember that your suffering is normal, and that it will heal as time passes. Only time can heal the deep pain you have experienced, and only time will show you what the inner meaning of this sad event is for you.

Soon you will be faced with some more tough decisions. If you choose to try again, I sincerely hope that you will be successful. If you choose to adopt, I wish you all the best. And if you choose to remain childless, I hope that you find fulfillment in the many other avenues that are now open to us as women. Whatever you decide, consider it carefully and make sure that it is the right decision for you, whatever that may be. Don't let others influence you—follow your instincts and your heart. That way, you will be at peace with your choice.

As a final word of advice, if you find yourself working too hard on your healing, to the point that it becomes stressful, take a break for some time and focus on other areas of your life. It is possible, after all, to become too focused on healing—which can have the opposite effect and actually delay your recovery process.

If you know of others who are suffering, make sure they know about my site and book. Most importantly, however, ensure that they are not alone in this difficult time. My purpose and mission is to help as many people as I can. It is my most sincere hope that you are one of them!

Together, we can help ourselves and other women through the pain of miscarriage. We can become stronger and wiser. Good luck with your own journey and know that I am right beside you in spirit. You are not alone.

APPENDIX

Surviving Miscarriage—A 30-Day Journal

INTRODUCTORY NOTE

In my book, "Surviving Miscarriage—You are Not Alone," I discussed at length how important and helpful it can be to be to keep a journal after your experience of a miscarriage. There are many reasons why journaling can be so therapeutic and such a powerful tool in the journey to overcome your grief.

For one thing, journaling can be a way of "talking out" your innermost emotions, even when you may not want to talk to friends, family members or even a professional therapist. Writing in a journal can give you a similar feeling of being able to purge your inner demons, with the added bonus that you can do it as often as you would like and confess even things you wouldn't want to if you were talking to a friend, parent or sibling.

A second benefit is that keeping track of your emotions and your environments can help you identify what triggers your good moods and what shifts you back into a bad mood.

Third, a journal is a way to get in touch with thoughts that may be buried deep down within your soul. As I explain in my book, rational-emotive and cognitive therapists believe that thoughts lead to feelings, which then lead to behaviors. By writing in a journal, you force yourself to focus on your thoughts, thus managing your feelings and behaviors more effectively. Since much of what we think is deeply ingrained in our subconscious, becoming automatic and second nature, we rarely stop to consider them carefully. Writing in a journal lets us "grasp" our thoughts and analyze them. Being able to view our thoughts in this way is a crucial step on the road to recovery.

I am providing you with this 30-day journal as motivation and incentive for you to keep a diary of your thoughts, emotions and the stage of grief that you are passing through at this point. Think of it as a map of your progress.

For each page, simply fill in the date, write down your emotions, and then identify the stage of grief as explained in the companion book. To refresh your memory, the five stages of grief are:

1.   Denial

2.   Anger

3.   Bargaining

4.   Depression/Anxiety

5.   Acceptance

Later, when you have gone through a 30-day cycle, look over your entries and assess your progress. Have you been cycling back and forth through particular stages? Are you moving forward? Is there a stage in which you appear "stuck?"

Take this journal in with you if you meet with a therapist, or let it be a sort of self-therapy. Whichever method you choose, just be sure to enter your feelings on a daily basis. Keeping to a schedule will not only help you get your life back on track, it will also enable you to have a more accurate view of your healing process.

I still keep a journal, to this day, of my thoughts and feelings. If you are not sure you are making progress in your healing, go back and re-read some of your earlier journal entries, like I do. You will amaze yourself at how much progress you truly have made.

As always, I wish you the best of luck during this process, however, more importantly, I wish you peace and healing.

Dr. Stacey J. McLaughlin

DAY 1

Date: _____/_____/_____

Emotions of the Day: _____

_____

_____

_____

Stage of Grief: _____

Special Events of the Day: _____

_____

_____

_____

General Notes: _____

_____

_____

_____

_____

_____

_____

_____

_____

DAY 2

Date: _____/_____/_____

Emotions of the Day: _____
_____
_____
_____

Stage of Grief: _____

Special Events of the Day: _____
_____
_____
_____

General Notes: _____
_____
_____
_____
_____
_____
_____
_____
_____

DAY 3

Date: _____/_____/_____

Emotions of the Day: _____
_____
_____
_____

Stage of Grief: _____

Special Events of the Day: _____
_____
_____
_____

General Notes: _____
_____
_____
_____
_____
_____
_____
_____
_____

DAY 4

Date: _____/_____/_____

Emotions of the Day: _____
_____
_____
_____

Stage of Grief: _____

Special Events of the Day: _____
_____
_____
_____

General Notes: _____
_____
_____
_____
_____
_____
_____
_____
_____
_____

DAY 5

Date: _____/_____/_____

Emotions of the Day: _____

_____

_____

_____

Stage of Grief: _____

Special Events of the Day: _____

_____

_____

_____

General Notes: _____

_____

_____

_____

_____

_____

_____

_____

_____

DAY 6

Date: _____/_____/_____

Emotions of the Day: _____
_____
_____
_____

Stage of Grief: _____

Special Events of the Day: _____
_____
_____
_____

General Notes: _____
_____
_____
_____
_____
_____
_____
_____
_____

DAY 7

Date: _____/_____/_____

Emotions of the Day: _____
_____
_____
_____

Stage of Grief: _____

Special Events of the Day: _____
_____
_____
_____

General Notes: _____
_____
_____
_____
_____
_____
_____
_____
_____
_____

DAY 8

Date: _____/_____/_____

Emotions of the Day: _____
_____
_____
_____

Stage of Grief: _____

Special Events of the Day: _____
_____
_____
_____

General Notes: _____
_____
_____
_____
_____
_____
_____
_____
_____

DAY 9

Date: _____/_____/_____

Emotions of the Day: _____
_____
_____
_____

Stage of Grief: _____

Special Events of the Day: _____
_____
_____
_____

General Notes: _____
_____
_____
_____
_____
_____
_____
_____
_____

DAY 10

Date: _____/_____/_____

Emotions of the Day: _____
_____
_____
_____

Stage of Grief: _____

Special Events of the Day: _____
_____
_____
_____

General Notes: _____
_____
_____
_____
_____
_____
_____
_____
_____

DAY 11

Date: _____/_____/_____

Emotions of the Day: _____

_____

_____

_____

Stage of Grief: _____

Special Events of the Day: _____

_____

_____

_____

General Notes: _____

_____

_____

_____

_____

_____

_____

_____

_____

DAY 12

Date: _____/_____/_____

Emotions of the Day: _____
_____
_____
_____

Stage of Grief: _____

Special Events of the Day: _____
_____
_____
_____

General Notes: _____
_____
_____
_____
_____
_____
_____
_____
_____

DAY 13

Date: _____/_____/_____

Emotions of the Day: _____
_____
_____
_____

Stage of Grief: _____

Special Events of the Day: _____
_____
_____
_____

General Notes: _____
_____
_____
_____
_____
_____
_____
_____
_____
_____

DAY 14

Date: _____/_____/_____

Emotions of the Day: _____
_____
_____
_____

Stage of Grief: _____

Special Events of the Day: _____
_____
_____
_____

General Notes: _____
_____
_____
_____
_____
_____
_____
_____
_____

DAY 15

Date: _____/_____/_____

Emotions of the Day: _____
_____
_____
_____

Stage of Grief: _____

Special Events of the Day: _____
_____
_____
_____

General Notes: _____
_____
_____
_____
_____
_____
_____
_____
_____

DAY 16

Date: _____/_____/_____

Emotions of the Day: _____
_____
_____
_____

Stage of Grief: _____

Special Events of the Day: _____
_____
_____
_____

General Notes: _____
_____
_____
_____
_____
_____
_____
_____
_____
_____

DAY 17

Date: _____/_____/_____

Emotions of the Day: _____
_____
_____
_____

Stage of Grief: _____

Special Events of the Day: _____
_____
_____
_____

General Notes: _____
_____
_____
_____
_____
_____
_____
_____
_____
_____

DAY 18

Date: _____/_____/_____

Emotions of the Day: _____
_____
_____
_____

Stage of Grief: _____

Special Events of the Day: _____
_____
_____
_____

General Notes: _____
_____
_____
_____
_____
_____
_____
_____
_____
_____

DAY 19

Date: _____/_____/_____

Emotions of the Day: _____
_____
_____
_____

Stage of Grief: _____

Special Events of the Day: _____
_____
_____
_____

General Notes: _____
_____
_____
_____
_____
_____
_____
_____
_____

DAY 20

Date: _____/_____/_____

Emotions of the Day: _____
_____
_____
_____

Stage of Grief: _____

Special Events of the Day: _____
_____
_____
_____

General Notes: _____
_____
_____
_____
_____
_____
_____
_____
_____

DAY 21

Date: _____/_____/_____

Emotions of the Day: _____

_____

_____

_____

Stage of Grief: _____

Special Events of the Day: _____

_____

_____

_____

General Notes: _____

_____

_____

_____

_____

_____

_____

_____

_____

DAY 22

Date: _____/_____/_____

Emotions of the Day: _____
_____
_____
_____

Stage of Grief: _____

Special Events of the Day: _____
_____
_____
_____

General Notes: _____
_____
_____
_____
_____
_____
_____
_____
_____

DAY 23

Date: _____/_____/_____

Emotions of the Day: _____

_____

_____

_____

Stage of Grief: _____

Special Events of the Day: _____

_____

_____

_____

General Notes: _____

_____

_____

_____

_____

_____

_____

_____

_____

DAY 24

Date: _____/_____/_____

Emotions of the Day: _____
_____
_____
_____

Stage of Grief: _____

Special Events of the Day: _____
_____
_____
_____

General Notes: _____
_____
_____
_____
_____
_____
_____
_____
_____

DAY 25

Date: _____/_____/_____

Emotions of the Day: _____
_____
_____
_____

Stage of Grief: _____

Special Events of the Day: _____
_____
_____
_____

General Notes: _____
_____
_____
_____
_____
_____
_____
_____
_____

DAY 26

Date: _____/_____/_____

Emotions of the Day: _____
_____
_____
_____

Stage of Grief: _____

Special Events of the Day: _____
_____
_____
_____

General Notes: _____
_____
_____
_____
_____
_____
_____
_____
_____

DAY 27

Date: _____/_____/_____

Emotions of the Day: _____
_____
_____
_____

Stage of Grief: _____

Special Events of the Day: _____
_____
_____
_____

General Notes: _____
_____
_____
_____
_____
_____
_____
_____
_____

DAY 28

Date: _____/_____/_____

Emotions of the Day: _____
_____
_____
_____

Stage of Grief: _____

Special Events of the Day: _____
_____
_____
_____

General Notes: _____
_____
_____
_____
_____
_____
_____
_____
_____
_____

DAY 29

Date: _____/_____/_____

Emotions of the Day: _____

_____

_____

_____

Stage of Grief: _____

Special Events of the Day: _____

_____

_____

_____

General Notes: _____

_____

_____

_____

_____

_____

_____

_____

_____

DAY 30

Date: _____/_____/_____

Emotions of the Day: _____
_____
_____
_____

Stage of Grief: _____

Special Events of the Day: _____
_____
_____
_____

General Notes: _____
_____
_____
_____
_____
_____
_____
_____
_____
_____

978-0-595-35636-2
0-595-35636-2

Made in the USA
Middletown, DE
01 September 2018